D0177823

000000591869

THE ART & CRAFT OF MAKING

CHILDREN'S
FURNITURE

DUDLEY PUBLIC LIBRARIES	
000000591869	
Bertrams	23/01/2013
684.104	£16.00
	SED

T H E **A** R T & **C** R A F T O F **M** A K I N G

CHILDREN'S
F U R N I T U R E

A Practical Guide,
with Step-by-Step
Instructions

CHRIS
SIMPSON

STOBART
DAVIES

A QUARTO BOOK

Copyright © 1995 Quarto Publishing plc

First published in Great Britain in 1995 by

STOBART DAVIES LIMITED
Priory House, Priory Street, Hertford, Herts SG14 1RN

This book may not be reproduced in whole or in part in any form or by any means,
electronic or mechanical, including photocopying, recording, or by any information,
storage and retrieval system now known or hereafter invented, without written
permission from the publisher and copyright holder.

A catalogue record for this book is available from the British Library
ISBN 0 85442 064 9

Designed and produced by

QUARTO PUBLISHING PLC, THE OLD BREWERY
6 BLUNDELL STREET, LONDON N7 9BH

SENIOR EDITOR	MARIA MORGAN
SENIOR ART EDITOR	MARK STEVENS
COPY EDITOR	REBECCA MYRAM
DESIGNER	STEVE MCCURDY
PHOTOGRAPHERS	IAN HOWES, PAUL FORRESTER
ILLUSTRATORS	DAVE KEMP, CHRIS ORR
ART DIRECTOR	MOIRA CLINCH
EDITORIAL DIRECTOR	MARK DARTFORD

Typeset by Central Southern Typesetters, Kent
Manufactured in Hong Kong by Regent Publishing Services Ltd
Printed in China by Leefung-Asco Printers Ltd

Publisher's note:
Woodworking can be dangerous. Both hand and power tools can quickly sever nerves, tendons or limbs. Always exercise extreme caution when working with wood.
Always read tool instruction manuals, use the safety guards provided, and wear protective gear and clothing. For illustrative purposes, many of these steps were omitted,
but this is not recommended operating procedure. As far as the methods and techniques mentioned in this book are concerned, all statements, information and advice
given are believed to be true and accurate. However, neither the authors, copyright holder, nor the publisher can accept any legal liability for errors or omissions.
The items shown in this book are the copyright of the individual makers and may not be reproduced for commercial purposes.

Contents

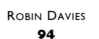

How to use this book

The book contains ten projects, each having a picture of the piece of furniture, plans and further information detailing the size, then a list of materials needed and a series of

photographs which describe the making process from start to final decoration. There are also illustrations of alternative decorative treatments. In addition, materials and techniques

sections cover general matters relating to most of the projects.

The projects were originated by designers and sometimes made by themselves or sometimes by other craftspeople.

This gives a different approach to each project and they vary from fairly simple to quite complex. In addition to the basic design and decoration used in these projects there is a section that

shows how the design may be adapted or customized to give different decorative approaches. This provides a guide so that you can follow our suggestions or make your

The ten projects are presented so that you can work through the book, learning and developing various skills and techniques as you progress through the more complex items.

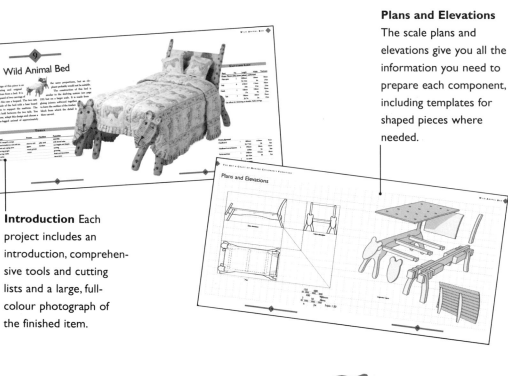

Introduction Each project includes an introduction, comprehensive tools and cutting lists and a large, full-colour photograph of the finished item.

Plans and Elevations
The scale plans and elevations give you all the information you need to prepare each component, including templates for shaped pieces where needed.

own adaptations.

If you take the latter route, stimulate your child's imagination and look for interesting subjects. Children may have their own ideas or you can fine inspiration from cartoons, nursery rhymes and various forms from the natural and man-made world. The choice of subjects is so vast that the only limitation is your imagination. If you do not feel you want to try your own ideas, adapt or adopt our suggestions.

Colour is important for children: again the child's own interests may guide you. Generally children like bright colours but subtler tones may be appropriate for older children. Mix patterns and textures with colour; good examples of this are the clown wardrobe and the toy box. Where a piece or component is shaped, we have suggested specific shapes, for instance the back and arms of the rocking chair but some of these could be altered to suit your own ideas.

Alternative Themes

Colour illustrations show a range of alternative designs and decorative treatments for each project to inspire you to adapt and customize the basic design to suit your own child.

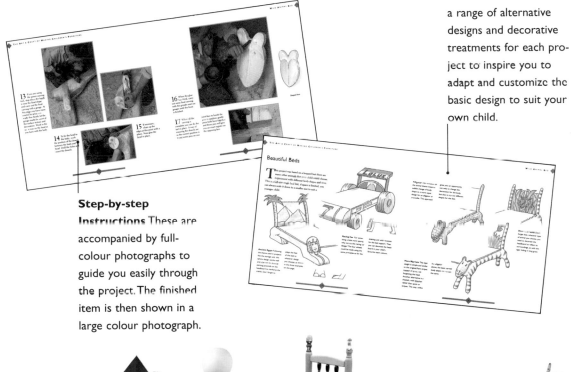

Step-by-step Instructions
These are accompanied by full-colour photographs to guide you easily through the project. The finished item is then shown in a large colour photograph.

Safety

When designing and making children's furniture it is very important to consider how it will be used and to make it as safe as possible. The projects in this book have been designed for different age ranges and of course it is possible, if you are considering any of the pieces for a particular age of child, to adjust the scale to suit.

In general there are two main areas concerning safety in use. First, try to ensure that a child cannot hurt him or herself on the furniture. For this reason many of the sharp edges have been rounded. The toybox is a good example of quite substantial rounding of the edges in order to avoid cuts or bruises. Most of the pieces in the book apply rounding to a certain extent and, generally, the younger the child, the greater the radius. The second point is stability. Again the furniture is designed to ensure safety in this respect. For example, we recommend that the runners on the crib be shaped or provided with stops so that it cannot rock too far.

Another element to consider is the toxicity of paint or other finishes. Fortunately, lead paint is not generally available now and most current finishes should not give any problems. When choosing a finish you have not tried before make sure that it is inert and will be safe when applied.

Safety should also be paramount during the actual making of the furniture so always follow good working practices. Hand tools can be dangerous if not properly used so follow normal woodworking procedures when using edge tools. Always work tools away from you and be aware of the position of your hands when holding the work and manipulating the tools.

With hand tools such as chisels, planes and saws, the sharper you keep them, the safer they are. A blunt tool requires more effort in use and the resulting overpressure can cause slips and therefore accidents. A sharp tool should cut the wood efficiently and safely, but always be aware of what is happening. The same principle of sharpness applies with power and machine tools. It is more dangerous to use tools which are blunt because their cutting action is impaired and the tendency is to force the material and this is when accidents can happen. Power and machine tools should always be used with the guards provided, although in the book you will see that we have occasionally removed the guards to make the photography clearer. This is, however, not recommended in practice.

Finally, always keep your working area tidy. Offcuts of wood, dust etc. can make floor surfaces slippery and of course the presence of waste can be a fire hazard. It is advisable never to smoke in your workshop and never undertake machining operations when you are tired or suffering from the effects of alcohol or some medication.

Drawings

The photographs at the start of each project show the different designs, so decide on a subject that will suit the child and that you feel happy to make. There are drawings and plans for each project and in some cases, templates for shaped pieces. Basically drawings are two-dimensional representations of the three-dimensional object and draughtsmen use the following conventions: plans, i.e. a view from the top; elevations, which are generally a view from the front or side; sections, where the piece is drawn as if it has been cut through to show hidden detail. These different views are laid out so that each refers to the other and the projections give an effective representation of the object.

The projection shown is called "first angle". Imagine the playhouse suspended in a square corner with a base and two "walls". As you look at each of the three faces imagine these being projected back onto the three surfaces so that the view that you see is represented on those surfaces. If you then cut along one corner and open it flat there are three views that represent three faces and they line up with one another. In this illustration the three faces are called front elevation, side (or end) elevation and plan. Often by drawing only the outsides, not all the necessary information is shown, so make another elevation as if the object had been cut. This is called the section and in this case the cut is made through the centre line. In some cases it may be more convenient to make this section in a different place and, if this is done, the position of the cut needs to be shown, i.e. section through A-A (either complete or a part as shown). The scale of the drawing may be such that more information needs to be shown so a detail is drawn to a larger scale. Sometimes it is necessary to show more than three sides which is possible using the same principle and all views or elevations relate to one another.

Plan

Unfold flat

Side elevation

Front elevation   Side elevation

Side section on centre line

Plan

Inverted plan

Rear elevation   Side   Front elevation   Side   Side section

Plan

Scale and dimensions

To be useful, any technical drawing must be drawn to scale and the scale or scales should always be indicated and the actual dimensions shown on the drawing. For most purposes there are accepted scales in general use and it is not wise to use "odd" scales. The main accepted scales are full or actual size, larger than full size or smaller than full size. For instance, full size is 1:1 or 1m = 1m or 1ft = 1ft. Larger scales than the object are used when the object is small and, for clarity, need to be drawn larger than reality. These can be twice full size, 2:1, 20mm = 10mm or 12in = 6in or another larger ratio can be chosen if necessary. Scales smaller than the object are mostly used when it is inconvenient or impossible to draw the object full size. Various scales are used: in metric 1:5, ⅕ full size or 1cm = 5cm, then scales 1:10, 1:20, 1:50, 1:100 and so on; in imperial 1:4, one-quarter full size or ¼in = 1in or 3in = 1ft, then

scales 1:12, 1:24, 1:48 etc. A drawing may have several different items at different scales, so the first thing to look for on any drawing is the scale(s) used.

The projects are also represented in the form of exploded drawings, but the actual details of components or parts of the furniture are shown on scaled grids. This works well, for instance, in the Humpty Dumpty stool, since turning is a very direct technique and generally only overall dimensions are needed. The detailed shape of the turning or other component is shown on a scaled grid which may, for example, be 1:5 with 5mm (³⁄₈in) squares. First draw an enlarged grid full size, i.e. draw each square shown on the page five times the size. Plot the major junctions from the grid in the book onto your full size grid and draw in the shape shown. Sometimes you will need to enlarge the book's drawings to make card or plywood templates as a guide for turning, for marking out the decoration or for cutting

shapes and components. If you are unhappy with plotting the junctions from the grid, you could photocopy the grid and enlarge it to the required size. Some older photocopiers only enlarge from sheet sizes, i.e. A4 to A3, but modern machines have a percentage increase.

Marking from plans

Grids have already been mentioned but on most of the pieces marking out should be a simple matter using pencils and rules. It is normal to use a pencil line for general marking and a cut line with a knife where you are going to saw.

Materials

Those not conversant with woodwork may not be aware of the woodworker's use of the terms "hardwood" and "softwood". These are not references to whether a wood is hard or soft, but are in fact botanical descriptions. Hardwoods are generally from broadleaved deciduous trees which often shed their leaves in the winter and softwoods come from evergreen trees which usually have needles rather than leaves. Balsa is in fact a hardwood but is very soft and yew is botanically a softwood but is quite hard and brittle. Remember this when purchasing your timber.

Many of the projects are designed to use manufactured board rather than solid timber. Many different types are made but you will probably find the following readily available. Boards made from solid timber include plywoods, where the board is composed of alternate layers of thin wood veneer glued together to form thicknesses ranging from 3, 4 and 6mm, up to

25mm and blockboard, which is made of strips of solid timber with constructional veneer on the outside faces.

The other type of board is particle board where the timber is reduced to its chips or fibres and then reconstituted into a board material. You will come across chipboard where you can see the nature of the chips and their cementing resin on the face and on the edges. The other common material is fibreboard, most recently Medium Density Fibreboard, commonly known as MDF. The advantage of this over chipboard is that the consistency of the fibres is much more even and you can achieve as good a finish on the edges as on the faces, whereas with chipboard you will always have to fill or lip the edges. Chipboard is also less satisfactory when screwing into the edges. Few particle boards are good for external use but plywoods come in several different qualities, some specifically made for outside or marine use.

The Playhouse is constructed from this material, the Toybox of interior grade multiply, and many of the other pieces from MDF.

Some of the furniture is made from solid timber and when using timber you can highlight the natural colours, patterns and textures that are available in different woods by applying oil or a clear lacquer finish. Remember it is preferable to use hardwoods in cases where you want the timber to be shown in its natural state. One major problem with solid timber is that when used for large surfaces there is a great deal of movement, particularly across the grain, and a board that was initially flat could warp. This is why most of the carcase or panel designs in this book use one of the manufactured boards. Solid timber is generally available in planks where the grain runs lengthwise. Because of the structure of the timber cells there is very little movement along the grain, the most movement occurs across

the grain. When timber is machined into a board or panel, movement along that board or in its thickness is negligible, but in the width movement can be quite substantial. Depending on how well the timber was seasoned (timber when felled has a very high moisture content and its moisture has to be removed by drying or kilning) sometimes the moisture content is not reduced to the level where it will be stable in interior environments. Make sure that the timber is supplied to you at the correct moisture content or bring the planks indoors to a heated area so that the timber can "second season" in an environment similar to that where it will be used. The finishing of both these materials is covered in the Finishing and Decoration section.

"Found" materials

Don't neglect unusual sources, for example, if you need something like a cylindrical pole. You could use manufactured dowels or found items such as broom handles. Many joinery suppliers have specialist sections of wood that are available for the joinery trade; often these shapes could be useful, from triangular section or quarter round section for use as fillets, up to the range of most complex mouldings.

Triangular section

Moulded fillet

Quarter round

Plastics

These are generally quite difficult to use in a home workshop. They are very difficult to glue and each specific plastic requires a specific glue. Polythene is most difficult to join using adhesive and really needs the facility to be able to melt or weld it together. Double-sided adhesive tape is often useful for joining plastic, as long as it is reinforced with a mechanical fixing. In the Playhouse we advise the use of plastic sheet rather than glass as this is safer both during making and when used by children. Some of the projects also need upholstery foam which is not difficult to obtain. The supplier will cut this to size or it can be cut on a bandsaw. You will also need fabric to make the upholstery covers.

Metals

Other non-timber materials are also used in the projects. There will be times when you wish to use metal nuts and bolts. The Circus Wardrobe uses special fittings with an internal thread that matches the external thread or bolt. If you want continuous bolts, metal studding is normally available. This is basically a length of threaded rod to which normal nuts can be applied. You will find studding in a range of sizes with corresponding nuts and washers.

Metal studding

Internal thread fitting

Paints

You may use a wide range of paints or lacquers for decoration and the only thing you need to remember is that whatever type you decide to use, stick to that and do not change midway since some finishes can react with others and spoil the surface. For instance, polyurethane over cellulose will react quite badly and cause the initial surface to wrinkle. A simple formulation used on many of the pieces is normal house decoration paint such as water-based vinyl or emulsion. This is easy to mix, easy to apply and does not react with any clear lacquer top coat. Artists' acrylic colours are a good choice when painting the fine details. They come in a wide range of colours but you could mix your own from the basic primary colours and black and white. You can use oil-based decorative paints, but I find the vinyls or emulsions easier to work with. You can, of course, use industrial paints such as cellulose, acrylics, polyurethanes and other specialist lacquers. However, on the whole I would keep away from these unless you have wide experience of them. It is also quite feasible to use standard automobile spray paints, available in aerosol cans, and we have used these for the Shelving System. If you decide to use these make sure that the primer/sealer coat and the lacquer are compatible and that you do not change types of lacquers during the finishing process.

Paints Several types of paint are used in the projects, ranging from enamels used in modelmaking, to ordinary car body spray paint (below).

Equipment

You may be a highly skilled woodworker with your own workshop and a wide range of machines as well as power and hand tools or you may be a novice with few tools working in a room of your house, or part of the garage, doubling as your workshop. Most of the projects in the book are designed so that they can be made quite simply even though a few of them were made by designers and furniture makers with an extensive range of equipment. You should, however, be able to achieve very good resutls by adaptation and using your imagination. The skilled woodworker with all the necessary equipment should not find any of the projects too difficult. The list of tools featured in each project includes machine tools as well as simpler tools but machinery will help you to work quickly, accurately and safely. As a woodworker with a smaller workshop, much of your work will be with hand-powered tools and smaller machine tools. You will find that most of the work that we have carried out has been

achieved using such tools. In general terms most of the projects need nothing more complex than electric drill, jigsaw and possibly a router.

One project that does need a specific machine is the Humpty Dumpty Stool/Chair and for that you will need a lathe for making the shaped decorative pieces. It is possible to buy fairly simple accessories for an electric drill to be able to turn small details. Initially the wood can be made round by taking square stock, planing along its length firstly to an octagon and continuing until you have a cylindrical component. This can

then be put in the electric drill lathe for the final turning.

For those with little experience or equipment most of the projects are still achievable. The first thing is to equip yourself with a place to work, the basis for this should be a stout and firm table. I assume that the table will normally be used for other activities so first protect its surface. It is a good idea to cover it with a light cloth then some polythene sheeting, fixed in place with adhesive or masking tape. Then cut a piece of manufactured board, slightly larger than the table size and place this on top. One of the most useful things

that the equipped workshop will have is a vice, so it will be necesary to develop ways of holding material as you work. G-cramps can be used to hold components in place. When you are sawing make sure that the saw line is past the edge of the working board and also that you clear the table underneath when you are drilling. To save time order your material from a wood or board supplier already cut to the final size; starting with pieces nearer the final size will save a lot of effort.

Lathe work Work at a comfortable height, moving with the cutting tool and keeping your body balanced (left).

Lift the handle to start cutting

Notch each side of the bead

Hold the chisel upright

Techniques

Power and Machine Tools

If you already have machine tools you will be experienced enough to cope with any of the projects in this book. A good electric drill should be the first tool to start with, but if you are starting off you can purchase attachments for the electric drill that will convert it into other power woodworking tools. I find the jigsaw and the orbital sander attachments quite useful and the drill can also provide a basis for a first lathe. The next tool would be a jigsaw and, even though this is generally used to go round curves, it can be very useful simply for cutting up solid timber boards and manufactured panels. Third, a router takes over from specialist hand tools such as rebate or grooving (plough) planes that are no longer readily available. A small router with a selection of cutters can accomplish many useful tasks.

When designing these projects it has generally been the intention to suggest and demonstrate construction and making techniques which are as simple as possible so that they may be carried out by woodworkers who are new to the craft or who have little experience. If you are an advanced woodworker, there is of course no reason why you should not adopt more of a cabinet-making approach, particularly with items such as drawers. Joints are used when components have to be fitted together and jigs are made so that the joining system can be carried out effectively.

Planing

Planes are available in several sizes but for general use a small jack plane is sufficient. It is essential that you have equipment such as an oilstone to sharpen the blade regularly since the use of manufactured board can blunt an edge fairly quickly. If you are not used to planing take some time to practise and develop your control

and adjustment of the tool. In several of the projects it is necessary to smooth curved work and here a spokeshave is required. Again, its blade needs to be kept sharp and you need to spend a little time familiarizing yourself with the tool.

Sharpening

For planes and chisels the sharpening stone is normally carborundum and needs to be lubricated with light machine oil. You will see that both tools have an angle which is ground and a slightly steeper angle which is honed on the stone. To sharpen put oil on the stone, rub the edge to be honed up and down the stone, making sure that you maintain the correct angle and a square edge. You will find that this action causes a small burr to appear on the flat side of the blade. When this has happened, carefully turn the blade over and with one or two strokes remove the burr. You should now find that you have a sharp edge.

Sawing

Many of the tool lists refer to a panel saw and if you have limited equipment this is a primary requisite since most of the general sawing can be accomplished with this tool. Some of the projects also need some finer sawing so for general use a small tenon saw is advisable. A panel saw is used for sawing through panel components and so this has no back to interrupt this process. The tenon saw, however, has a metal back, usually brass, which holds the saw blade rigid. Obviously this is meant for cuts which do not go through the material or for sawing thin materials. When sawing curves, there are several saws available, the two I would recommend are the coping saw and the pad or keyhole saw. The coping saw enables you to cut quite tight curves but the depth of the throat of the saw limits the distance away from the edge to which you can cut. The pad saw is designed for working

away from the edge but can only cut gentle curves. Both these saws need an initial hole drilled in the material to put the blade through before cutting. You will find, however, that sawing thick material will be a slow job.

Chiselling

The craftsman will have a wide range of chisels but you should be able to manage with three – a narrow one about 6mm (¼in), a medium one about 12mm (½in) or 16mm (⅝in) and a wider one about 19–25mm (¾–1in). Again, practise producing a keen edge on the tool.

Drilling

Most of the projects need drilling in some form or other, either for insertion of screws, drilling for dowels or drilling larger circular components as used in the Rocking Chair and the Humpty Dumpty Chair. If you have no machine tools, a small wheel brace is fine for the smaller holes but for larger ones you really need a brace and set of bits. If you are using power or machine tools a wide range of twist drills from 2mm (1/16in) to 12mm (1/2in) and over are available. For woodwork I normally prefer the larger ones to have a centre spur. Note when inserting screws always drill pilot holes – a larger one for the shank and a smaller one for the screw thread itself. You will also need a countersink.

In many of the projects you will need to drill holes that do not go right through the material so it is necessary to make some form of depth stop. On the illustration of the little rocking chair you will see the idea of putting some masking tape around the drill at the required depth. This is an effective method but when drilling a lot of holes it is easy to damage the tape, so you need to check it frequently. Attachments can be purchased which can be fitted to drills but you can easily make a depth stop yourself by taking a piece of dowel, drilling it through the centre and cutting it to a length so that one end rests against the chuck, leaving the required projection of the drill bit that corresponds to the depth of the hole required. Simple drilling jigs are also used when drilling at angles.

Using masking tape as a depth stop

Drilling through from both sides

Hold dowels in a v-shaped block when drilling

Joints

Having prepared these materials for assembly, we need to determine how we will approach jointing.

Many of the projects use glue and screws, some of them use methods that will be familiar to the competent woodworker. Alternative jointing systems can be quite simple but, of course, the woodworker likes to keep up with technology. The Circus Wardrobe shows the use of the biscuit jointer where a special circular saw makes slots into which specially made "biscuits" are inserted. These make very strong joints in cabinet construction since not only do the biscuits fit snugly in the groove, but they swell slightly when glue is applied. However, if you do not have the equipment for this, don't worry, there are two other, simpler ways available. If you have a router you can make grooves into which you can fit tongues. Tongues are normally cut from plywood so if you use a thickness of 4mm (1/8in) with a 4mm router cutter, you have a very effective tongue and groove jointing method. If you don't have a router, the traditional method of using dowels is simple and effective. Mark out the centres of the dowels on one component, select your dowel size and appropriate drill then drill the holes. Now use dowel pins (it is worth investing in a set of these) to transfer the position of these holes. Put these into the holes you have already drilled, line up the other part of the joint by pressing or lightly cramping the joint together and the dowel centre will be marked on the other face. Drill the matching holes. This method should ensure accurate jointing. Other joints used include mortise, halving joints and lap joints.

Dowel joint

Halving joint

Routing grooves Plunge the router to the maximum depth, move smoothly to the end of the groove, switch off and then lift the router off the work.

Mechanical fixings

We have made much use of screws, either with glue for assembly, or to fix other fixtures and fittings. Screws can now be found with many different threads and heads. The main heads you will come across will be either countersunk or roundhead, the former being used where you wish the screw to be level with the surface. Screwdrivers have two common driving heads – the traditional slot and the star-shaped or crosshead type. Three types of screw thread are generally available: the traditional screw with a third shank and two-thirds thread; screws where the thread runs the whole length of the screw and also special screws for fixing manufactured board. Some of the pieces use nails or pins and, as with screws, there are many different types and sizes. As well as these "connection" devices, the projects use other common fittings including hinges and castors.

Adhesives

All of the projects specify the use of a glue or adhesive but there are various types used in woodworking. You will come across the following glues available under many different trade names. PVA glue has a white creamy texture and spreads easily; it is ideal for internal work and has been used in most of the projects in this book. There are many different formulations so you should easily find one to suit your purposes. Another glue commonly available to furniture makers is UF (Urea Formaldehyde). In small quantities this comes as a powder which you have to mix with water to the correct consistency and is useful where some degree of moisture resistance is necessary. It is essential to get the mixing consistency correct or the glue's bonding effectiveness will be reduced. There are some two-part UF glues which consist of a resin and a hardener, sometimes a powder and a liquid or sometimes

two liquids. These and other specialist resins, however, will be more difficult to find than PVAs and the powder UFs, since many of the adhesives used in the furniture industry are not generally available. You may need to consider epoxies which are used to join metal and other materials, and also to use contact or impact glues. These are normally rubber based, they are spread on both surfaces to be joined, and after a short period of drying are brought together to make a firm joint. These adhesives have been used on some of the items with upholstery.

Cramping

Cramps are either used to hold work or to help assembly and the most useful type is the G-cramp which suits both purposes. You will need at least half a dozen of these and some of them should be the one-handed type which are more for holding than assembly. Sash cramps are also necessary; for most of the work small ones, 76cm (2ft 6in), will suffice but I advise 3 or 4.

Cramping Use sash cramps to hold glued sections, checking that frames are square with a try square and ruler for the diagonals.

Finishing and Decoration

Prior to final decoration all surfaces need to be cleaned and then sealed. First clean with abrasive paper; at this stage it is a good idea to use garnet paper which is available in many grits, from coarse to very fine. When using manufactured board you should only ever need to lightly sand the pieces with a medium to fine grit paper, but you may also have to fill edges, recess screw holes and pin holes so you may need a coarser grade paper to get these flat.

Abrasives

When we think of abrasives as used in woodwork, the usual term used is "sandpaper". Abrasive papers, however, do not use sand as a grit, but other minerals such as glasspaper. This is generally used for joinery work and not fine woodworking. Garnet paper is the material most often used by cabinet makers. Aluminium oxide paper is often used with power tools. Silicon carbide paper is used by metal workers as "wet and dry" paper, but furniture makers use a self lubricating type. Used dry it is ideal for rubbing down lacquer. Steel wool can be used in its fine grades for final finishing. Abrasive papers come in several grades which are expressed by the coarseness of the grit, ranging from 50, which is the coarsest, down to 600, which is the finest. Remember that when the text refers to "sanding" this means using abrasive paper.

You should not try to achieve a final finish by using abrasive paper instead of a plane or spokeshave. However, when solid timber surfaces have been smoothed, to get a good finish you need to use a fairly coarse paper first and work down through the grades. Generally, when working on flat surfaces, use a cork block to prevent the sandpaper causing ridges.

Sanding Use a sanding block on faces and edges or wrap the abrasive around a piece of dowel for sanding grooves. Finish with a finer grade.

Decoration

When the surface is ready, decide which decorative techniques you will use. If you have used solid timber and wish to show the natural grain and colour, then you will need to apply a clear lacquer which will both protect the wood and enhance the colour and grain. Apply a thin coat of clear lacquer first and when this is dry rub it down with abrasive paper such as silicon carbide. Use a fine grade which will enable you to produce a very good surface. Apply as many coats as you wish, rubbing down between each coat as described and finally use some very fine steel wool with a touch of wax polish for the final finish. You will find that this will give the timber a satin sheen.

If you are using natural timber but wish to enliven it with a colour stain, apply the stain before any lacquer. Always try the stain you wish to use on a spare scrap of the wood you have used since it can look different even when used on woods of the same species. You may have to experiment to get the colour you require. You can use either water or oil stains, but I would usually recommend a water stain if a lacquer is being applied over it. The water stain will raise the grain and you may have to rub down lightly again before applying a final coat of lacquer. It is possible to lacquer manufactured board but in all the projects in this book it has been used as a base for decoration. You should have little need to sand the faces but if using chipboard, you will need to finish the edges as I mentioned when writing about Manufactured Board. With man-made board you will need to apply a primer/sealer finish. This can be achieved by using an ordinary lacquer or ordinary paint, but there are specially formulated paints available which prime the surface for subsequent coats and fill minor defects. Apply this to the necessary surfaces and when dry lightly cut down with a fine abrasive paper. You should plan the decoration in stages starting with covering large areas and finishing with the fine details. This procedure is shown well in the Toybox where, after marking out with pencil, the base colours are brushed in.

Application

Most of the furniture in the book has used finishes which are applied with a brush and this is one of the easiest ways of application. You will need a variety of brushes to cover painting in large areas and to paint in the details. Always clean the brushes properly after use. Where you want to achieve a sharp line between two colours, you can use masking tape. This is shown in the Desk project. Make sure that the first surface is dry and hard before putting on the masking tape and, having painted the second colour, do not leave it on longer than is necessary. You can also use masking tape to paint curves by applying tape and cutting a curved edge with a sharp knife or scalpel.

Final decoration can be painted as shown in the Toybox, but you can also use other techniques. One of the rocking chairs uses "found" illustrations which were glued in position, extra paint applied to complete the

picture and the whole assembly sealed with clear lacquer when dry. On the crib we have used stencils which you can buy ready printed or you can make your own. As you will see from the stages in crib decoration, you need to cut the stencils very carefully, removing only the shapes which will be filled in with paint. Treat the whole stencil with a thin layer of linseed oil and when this has dried, it will stop the card softening when the paint is applied through the stencil.

On the painted version of the rocking chair we added surface decoration in the form of found illustrations. If you can find such illustrations and you don't mind cutting them out of books or magazines, you can use these but make sure that the paper on which the illustration is printed is sufficiently thick so that the print on the reverse will not show through when adhesive is applied and it is fixed in position. Alternatively, you can copy or trace the illustrations. Another

method is to photocopy them; colour photocopiers are becoming more accessible and illustrations can also be enlarged or reduced.

This describes the decorative treatments we have used in the book but there may be other effects which you would like to try such as marbling, combing, sponging, spattering, ragging etc. There are numerous books available which show how to achieve all these different effects.

Application Fine detail is painted in enamel for a sharp, vibrant finish (above). The cut-and-paste method (below) is simple but effective, as is sponging (right) to create a textured paint finish.

1

Cosy Rocking Crib

This is a simple but attractive piece of furniture for your baby's first few months. The construction is very easy, but the result is charming and can be decorated in many different ways. Some components are suited to manufactured board such as plywood, MDF or chipboard; remember that screws as well as glue will be used for assembly and the material needs to accept screw fixings into its edges. Some other components will be made from timber, and these include the base supports and the rockers.

TOOLS

Hand	Power	Machine	Function
Handsaw	jigsaw	bandsaw	cut out shapes
Plane			smooth straight edges
Spokeshaves/rasps			smooth curved edges
Hand drill	electric drill		drill holes for screws and dowels
Twist drills			drill holes for screws and dowels
Screwdriver			insert screws
Pin hammer			insert panel pins
Brushes			apply finish
Stencil brush			apply stencils

CUTTING LIST

Part	No	Length	Width	Thickness
From manufactured board				
Sides	2	675mm	600mm	12mm
		26½in	24in	½in
High end	1	700mm	480mm	12mm
		27½in	19in	½in
Low end	1	515mm	420mm	12mm
		20¼in	16½in	½in
Perforated base	1	630mm	360mm	12mm
		25in	14¼in	½in
From solid wood				
Base supports – long sides	2	625mm	20mm	20mm
		24½in	¾in	¾in
Base supports – short sides	2	325mm	20mm	20mm
		12¾in	¾in	¾in
Rockers	2	660mm	100mm	25mm
		26in	4in	1in
Canopy rail	1	480mm	60mm	25mm
		19in	2⅜in	1in
From hardboard or thin plywood				
Laminate for shaped canopy	3	545mm	250mm	3mm
		21½in	10in	⅛in
Wooden spheres	6			
Plus: Glue, screws, nails/pins, abrasive paper, filler, masking tape, primer/sealer, paints, stencils.				

Plans and Elevations

Side elevation

Front elevation

50   200

100   300mm

1   6   12ins

2   8   Scale 1:10

Plan

Templates

These templates are both half size, so scale them up and use the two halves of each template to produce the rockers and the top.

Exploded view

Cutting the shapes

1 Mark out the components. Cut rectangles before making shapes, curves or tapers, to make it easier to ensure that such shaping is regular around a centre line. Mark out and cut the rockers and the bed base support battens.

Rockers

2 Start with the two sides (one left- and one right-hand). The low (foot) end tapers to the base and has a rounded top. The high (head) end also tapers and the shaped top forms the crib canopy. The tapered ends support the bed base and form the rockers. Cut rectangles for the sides and ends, mark a centre line in each, and mark and then cut the long tapers. Repeat a similar operation on the sides, cutting tapers and making the low side and high end for the canopy.

3 Now assemble the ends. Mark the position of the rockers and bed base supports, screw the supports in place and then the rockers. The two ends stop short of the actual rocker curves so that the crib is supported only on the rockers, thus allowing the curve to be altered if required. The general sequence in most cases where a piece is screwed and glued together is: mark out, drill screw pilot hole, countersink when necessary; insert screws dry, check, if satisfactory, remove the screws; apply glue and finally fix together. Next, cut the shaped rail for the front of the canopy; the shape of this must match the one at the high end.

Assembly

4 To assemble the main structure, position and fix both sides to the vertically tapered edges of the ends. Fix the canopy rail in position using the sequence described earlier. Cut the perforated base to size and rest it in place to keep the structure square.

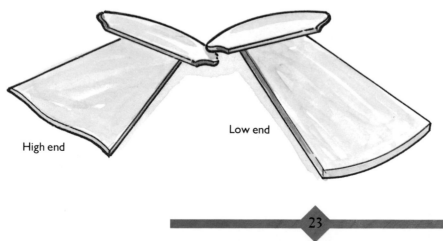

High end

Low end

5 This stage shows an interesting technique – that of forming the canopy shape. In industry, shapes such as these would need jigs and presses to accomplish, but for the home woodworker this result can be achieved in the following way. The thickness of the shaped canopy is approximately 9mm (⅜in). To make it yourself, use three sheets that are 3mm (⅛in) thick and able to bend easily to the required shape, such as hardboard or thin plywood. Spread glue onto the top edge of the high end, the top of the canopy rail and the tops of the two sides.

6 Position one of the thin sheets and hold it securely in place. Fix it to the end with panel pins. You can hold the sheet down to the shape using G-cramps while you fix it in position with panel pins.

◆ Creating curves

7 When the glue is dry, remove the cramps; the sheet will remain in the shape required. Apply glue to this formed surface and position the next sheet on this glued surface.

Cramp in position and insert more panel pins to hold. When the glue is dry, repeat this process with the final thin sheet to give a strong curved component.

9 Whichever way you make the spheres, apply glue and tap them into place. Repeat the procedure to fix the spheres at the foot end of the crib.

8 Carefully drill the holes to accept the dowels which are located in the decorative spheres. You should be able to purchase wooden spheres or, if you have turning equipment, you can make them yourself.

You can use any material to make the spheres, as long as they are drilled to accept the fixing dowels. Alternatively, use proprietary spheres such as door/drawer knobs of the correct size; these often have fixing screws already attached to them.

CROSS REFERENCE	
Laminating	14
Adhesives	15
Cramping	15

Finishing

10 To prepare the crib for finishing fill any screw holes, pin holes or rough edges with filler, then sand all the edges with abrasive paper as necessary.

11 The crib is now ready for decorating, but first check the rocking motion. This should not be too extreme as it could be dangerous, so either lessen the curve by planing, or screw small stops to the underside of the rockers at the end to limit the amount of travel.

12 Apply a white primer/filler coat and when this is dry apply your chosen colour of paint. Paint one colour first and, when this is dry, prepare the next colour.

13 Before painting the rest of the crib paint the decorative spheres. In order not to mark the painted surface, make a mask of paper to protect it while painting the spheres. Fold the paper twice, cut off the common corner and slit one edge; open out the paper and locate it around the base of the sphere.

15 First, cut out the stencil pattern carefully with a scalpel or sharp-pointed knife, making sure that you use a cutting board underneath to protect table surfaces.

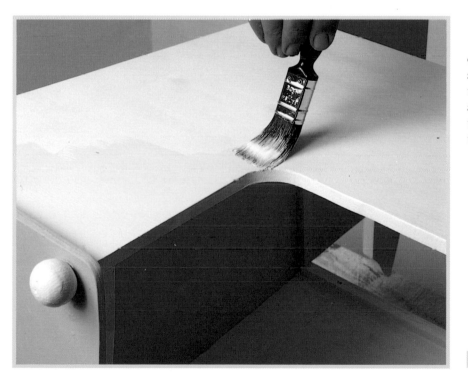

14 Then paint the rest of the crib in another colour – in this case yellow. When the base coats are dry the crib may be decorated with stencils. These are commercially available, although you could make your own.

CROSS REFERENCE

Paints	11
Finishing	17
Stencilling	17

16 Prepare the thin card on which the stencil pattern is printed by applying several coats of 50% linseed oil/50% turpentine to stiffen and protect the mask from the effects of applying paint with a stencil brush, which has very stiff bristles.

Stencilling

17 Before you apply the stencil to the crib itself, try a sample on a spare piece of board to get used to the process. Then hold the stencil in position on the crib with masking tape and stencil the yellow horse to the blue end first.

18 Remove the tape and reposition the stencil on the yellow side to apply a blue horse or one in a colour of your choice. Lift the stencil at one end to check your work. When the paint is dry, apply a coat of clear varnish to protect the decoration.

19 Now all that remains is to add the perforated base, a suitable mattress to fit and some bedding. The finished crib will be an invaluable part of your child's nursery.

Rock-a-bye Baby

The original crib was painted blue and yellow and then decorated with stencilled horses. Experiment with other colours and decorative finishes as in these examples, try making your own stencils or use the cut and paste method shown for the decorated version of the rocking chair.

Panelling Another way of achieving interesting effects is to add applied shapes to give a panelled effect. Another view of this is shown on the following page, with the panelling on the high and low ends of the crib.

Circus This follows the theme used for the wardrobe in the final project. Make the colours more vibrant with decorations of clowns, acrobats or animals and a striped canopy top.

Panelling Here we have another view of the shaped panels continued from the previous page. Try using different sizes and shapes for the panels for maximum effect.

Cutouts and Colours This is another effective decorative approach and here the heart cutout is contrasted with two colours. Use this idea with other shapes – simple circles, squares or triangles or with more complex shapes. However, do make sure that the structural rigidity of the piece is not compromised by the use of overlarge cutouts.

Natural Finishes Instead of manufactured board with veneer faces lipped with timber, this piece would look very good simply as natural wood. Carry this approach further by adding decorative effects to give a rustic or antique finish to the crib.

2

Desk and Stool Set

This useful little desk incorporates an upholstered stool so that a child can sit, write, paint or carry out other desk activities. This desk is designed for a young child around 4–7 years old, but a full-size one works just as well. The only requirement is to change the dimensions in proportion, remembering that the normal height of a table is between 700 and 750mm (27½ and 29½ inches). You can see how the parts are arranged on a standard sheet of manufactured board, so make sure you purchase enough board to cut all of the components. Use material of between 9 and 12mm (⅜ and ½in) since, even though it can be made with thinner material, the structure is held together by glue and screws and anything thinner than this may be difficult to screw into. Ordinary screws can be used, but it is better to purchase particle/ fibreboard screws which have a double thread and hold better in manufactured board.

TOOLS

Hand	Power	Machine	Function
Handsaw	circular saw	dimension saw	cut main components
Bowsaw/padsaw/coping saw	jigsaw	bandsaw	cut curves
Tenon saw	jigsaw	bandsaw	cut joints
Plane			smooth straight edges
Spokeshave			smooth curved edges
Chisel/file/rasps			smooth and fit joints
Hand drill	electric drill		drill and countersink screw holes
Twist drills and countersink bits			drill and countersink screw holes
Screwdriver			insert screws
Scissors			cut fabric
Needle and thread			sew fabric
Brushes/mops			apply finish

CUTTING LIST

Part	No	Length	Width	Thickness
From manufactured board				
Front	1	600mm	450mm	12mm
		24in	17¾in	½in
Top	1	600mm	450mm	12mm
		24in	17¾in	½in
Seat support panel	1	500mm	450mm	12mm
		19¾in	17¾in	½in
Shelves	2	500mm	250mm	12mm
		19¾in	10in	½in
Seat support crossrail	1	150mm	70mm	12mm
		6in	2¾in	½in
Fixed seat disk	1		160mm diam.	
			6¼in	
Upholstered disk	1		200mm diam.	
			8in	
Foam seat	1		200mm diam.	50mm
			8in	2in
Upholstery edging	1	600mm		40mm diam.
(pipe lagging)		24in		1½in diam.
Fabric seat cover	1		300mm diam.	
			12in	
Fabric seat edge	1	600mm	150mm	
		24in	6in	
Fabric rim	1	800mm	250mm	
		31½in	10in	

Plus: Abrasive paper and sanding block, screws, glue for wood, contact glue for foam and fabric, primer/sealer, paints, masking tape.

Plans and Elevations

Front elevation

Side elevation

Plan

50	200	
100	300mm	
1	6	12ins
2	8	

Scale 1:10

Templates

This template is for the main support of the desk.

Exploded view

Marking out

1 First, mark out the components on the board and cut them out roughly using a hand saw, hand-powered jigsaw or the combination of a circular saw/radial arm saw and bandsaw.

Cutting curves

2 Many pieces require rounded corners; you can use a compass to mark these, but it is often quicker and easier to draw round some form of cylinder such as a cup or bottle top. The advantage here is that you can place the object exactly in the corner and draw round it easily.

3 To mark and cut larger curves make two marks to indicate the ends of the curve and also the depth of the curve from the edge. Locate a panel pin at each of the end marks. Push a flexible rule into the curve to the required depth from the edge and draw a pencil line along the rule to mark the curve.

4 Cut the marked curve with a bandsaw. Alternatively, use a hand-powered jigsaw or a hand coping saw or hand padsaw.

5 The structure is made up of two shelves which are halved into the upright panel supporting the table top and the seat. Mark out the halvings and cut them on a bandsaw by making two parallel cuts. The waste can be removed with a chisel.

6 You may find that the halvings need to be adjusted slightly to make a precise fit; this can be done easily by using a rasp.

7 When the components are cut to size, start to assemble the unit. Fix the shelves into the main upright panel, along their halving joints. Then precisely locate the shelves and the upright onto the front of the desk. Measure to check that they are in exactly the correct position, and mark their position.

8 Remove the assembly and mark the position of the screws to join the front to the upright. Drill the holes for the screws from the marked positions on the inside of the front.

10 It is a good idea at this stage to bring the components together and, when correctly positioned, drill small pilot holes through the face into the edge of the manufactured board.

9 When all these holes have been drilled, turn the board over and countersink the holes so that the screw head will be flush with, or below, the finished surface.

Assembly

11 Now assemble part of the work. First, disassemble the shelves from the main upright, glue these joints, and slot them back together. The pilot holes indicate the screw positions. Now bring the face to the assembly and glue and screw the components together.

12 At this stage the assembled components can stand without support.

CROSS REFERENCE	
Drilling	13
Adhesives	15

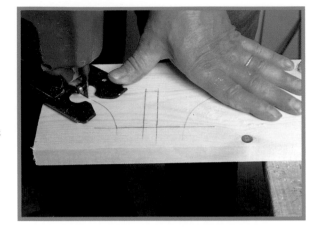

13 So that the seat can be securely fixed, make another cross halving joint. Make the seat support from a piece of softwood or from an offcut of the board material.

Seat support

14 Cut out the circular seat and also a piece of upholstery foam to fit. Inset the seat support into the halving cut into the upright and place the circular seat in position. Mark where you wish the screws to be and drill the holes. To assemble this part of the piece, spread the glue at the halving joint and locate firmly.

15 Finally, make the table top. Cut this to size, remove the semicircular cutout, then mark and cut out a small curve to remove the sharp corner. Smooth the corner with abrasive paper.

17 At this stage, sandpaper the edges to soften any sharp corners. The unit is now ready for finishing. Check that the upholstery foam sits in the correct place.

18 Use a piece of foam pipe insulation as a softening strip and apply this to the inside of the curve. Check that these upholstery components fit. Do not actually apply them with glue until the finishing process has been completed.

16 Repeat the dry assembly with the top, marking the screw holes using the same procedure shown for fixing the front face to the upright and shelves. Fit the top in position to the front top edge and the top of the upright and mark as before from the underside. Drill pilot holes and then turn to the outside face to countersink the screws. Assemble dry and, if satisfied, disassemble, glue and screw together. When this has been done, fix the seat. Apply glue to the seat support and put in place. Screw the seat disk into place.

CROSS REFERENCE	
Joints	14
Drilling	14
Sanding	16

19 Now the structure is complete, apply the white primer sealer to all the MDF surfaces. Do not paint the edge of the cutout and the top of the seat, as these will be upholstered.

22 When the paint has dried, very carefully remove the masking tape. The edges can now be painted with the bright yellow.

20 When the primer coat is dry, if you are decorating to the candy-striped design, apply an overall coat of the light yellow paint. Allow this to dry then add the bright blue paint to all horizontal surfaces.

21 To make the candy-striped design, mark out the position of the stripes and carefully apply masking tape to cover the area you wish to remain yellow. Then paint in the light blue on all the surfaces not masked on the appropriate pieces.

The upholstery

23 Here the fabric has been glued to the upholstery foam; although this works perfectly well, if you can use a sewing machine, the seatcover may be pre-sewn. Spread glue on the disk of upholstery foam and on the disk of MDF, and then bring these two surfaces together.

24 Next, apply some glue to the sides of the foam disk and to the edges of the fabric disk. Now place the fabric disk on top of the foam and pull the fabric down the sides and glue in place.

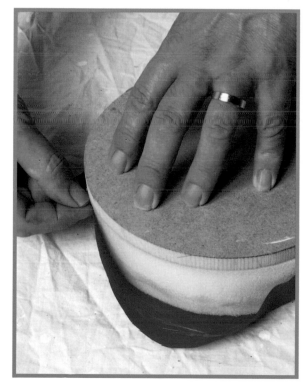

Using fabrics

25 To make an edge around the seat, first take some fabric, apply glue to the edge and fold it over to give a crisp edge that will not fray. Apply glue to the top of this strip and to the top edge of the fabric that has been pulled down over the foam disk. When the glue is tacky, apply the strip to the side of the seat.

26 Now turn the seat so that you can put some glue on the base and round the edge of the fabric and pull down, as shown, to make a neat finish. Glue the finished seat in position and leave to dry.

CROSS REFERENCE	
Painting	17
Adhesives	15

27 The upholstery for the cutout in the desk shape is carried out in a similar way. First make a strip, fold the edge as described for the seat, then glue this strip around the edge of the cutout.

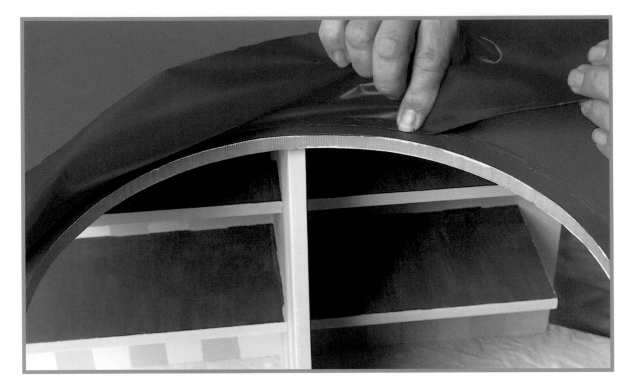

28 Spread glue onto the foam softening strip and position it round the cutout. Pull the fabric over the softening strip and glue it underneath. Make small circular pieces to tidy up the end detail here. If you are skilled with needle and thread the folded edges, which in this example are simply stuck with adhesive, can be slip-stitched both on the seat and on the softening strip. If you have a tacker, this could be used to apply the fabric around the edge of the top cutout.

29 The finished desk has plenty of workspace and, with the shelves tucked away underneath, is an extremely practical item for children of all ages.

Desk and Stool Sets

The prototype is shown in blue, red and yellow but there are many different approaches that will give interesting results. Not only can you scale up the size from the original, you can also experiment with different shapes for the top and a wide range of shelf and drawer arrangements. For older children, scale up for use as a computer workstation.

Apple This illustration shows the top curved and shaped to look like an apple with the cutout made to look like a bite. Decorate it with relevant illustrations such as leaves and even a smiling maggot.

Double Up Homework is much more fun, and a lot easier, when done with a friend, brother or sister and this "head-to-head" arrangement is ideal for lightening the load. This could also be the ideal arrangement when playing board games for two or more people, as others could sit round the sides.

Drawing Board Here an extra hinged surface is added to the top to serve as a drawing board for budding designers. Roughen the surface with something like felt and this arrangement will be just the thing for jigsaw puzzle enthusiasts.

Drawers and Cupboards Try adding some extra pieces to the shelves underneath to make drawers. Or even change the direction so that they open out to the side. Another option is to add doors to the shelves to make cupboards, as with the wardrobe project later in the book.

The Natural Look This could be achieved by using MDF, chipboard or plywood that has a timber veneered surface. The edges can then be filled and painted the same colour as the upholstery on the seat and desk rim. For very young children a small rail could be fitted to three sides on the top to stop things falling off.

Other Approaches Seats can take various forms and here we have a bicycle saddle, and a solid wood seat instead of upholstery. Or try using a large piece of threaded metal for an adjustable seat height, just like in a photo booth.

3

Train Toybox

This design combines simplicity in making with an interesting opening system that also enables it to be used for play. To make the application of hinged parts easy, a method similar to the one on the Playhouse is used. The box is made from 15mm (⅝in) multiply, though other manufactured board could be used, as long as it is thick enough and dense enough to take screws into its edge. If you use large enough castors, the toybox will be fully mobile when open, making playtime even more fun for your children.

TOOLS

Hand	Power	Machine	Function
Handsaw	circular/jigsaw	dimension saw	cut main components
Padsaw	jigsaw		cut openings
Plane			smooth straight edges
Spokeshave/rasps	router		work round edges
Hand drill	electric drill		drill and countersink screw holes
Twist drills and countersink bits			drill and countersink screw holes
Screwdriver			insert screws
Brushes/mops			apply finish

Part	No	Length	Width	Thickness
From 12mm (½in) multiplywood manufactured board				
Top	1	600mm	500mm	12mm
		24in	19¾in	½in
Bottom	1	600mm	500mm	12mm
		24in	19¾in	½in
Long sides	2	600mm	400mm	12mm
		24in	15¾in	½in
Short sides	2	500mm	400mm	12mm
		19¾in	15¾in	½in

Plus: Castors, hinges, glue, screws, masking tape, abrasive paper, sanding block, primer/sealer, paints.

Plans and Elevations

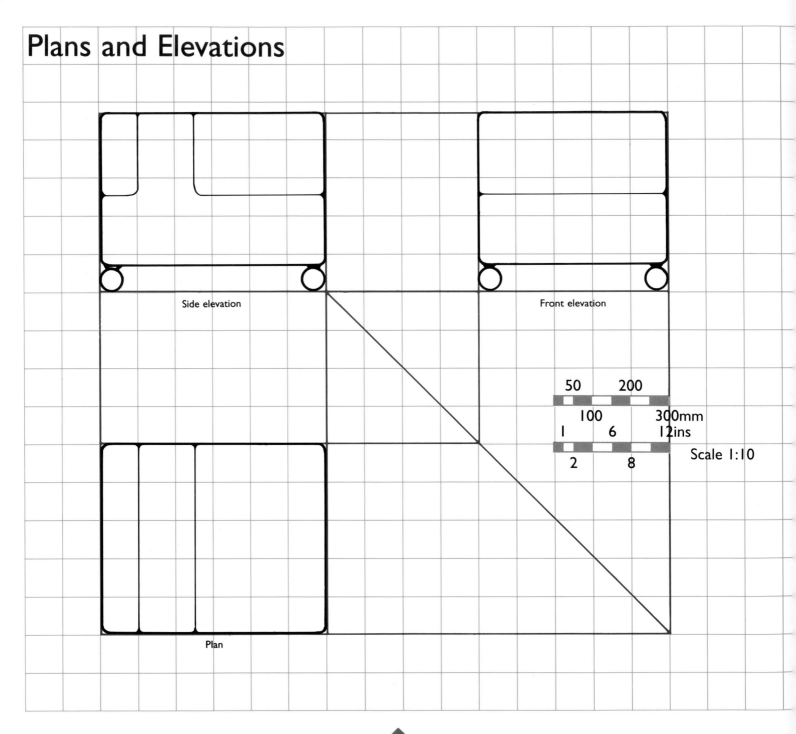

Side elevation

Front elevation

Plan

50	200
100	300mm
1	6	12ins
2	8

Scale 1:10

Exploded view

Making the box

1 The drawing shows the components required. Start by making a simple assembly of a six-sided box that is screwed together and later glued. Cut the six parts to the sizes shown and mark the positions where the screws are to be inserted. These are on the ends of the two long sides, and on all four sides of the top and bottom. Note that there is a particular arrangement of the screw positions around the area where the box will later be cut.

2 Drill all these positions with a twist drill that gives clearance for the screw shank and countersink the holes on the outside faces.

4 Now mark out in pencil where the lines are to be cut to enable the two parts of the box to open. Disassemble the box and make short sawcuts on the ends where the hinges are to be. These allow the jigsaw to be easily inserted when cutting the openings. Reassemble the box, this time applying glue to the joining surfaces before screwing together. When the glue is dry, you will have a strong box.

3 Locate the long sides in position on the ends, drill a pilot hole for each screw thread, and screw together. Next, place the top on this open box, drilling a pilot hole for each screw, and screw in place. Repeat this with the top and the bottom of the box. You now have a six-sided rectangular box that is temporarily screwed together.

5 Make sure that the joined edges are flush with the sides by planing off any slight projection.

CROSS REFERENCE	
Cutting curves	36
Drilling	14
Planing	13

The hinges

6 Now fit the hinges; if you follow this method and sequence you will have no problems with fitting and alignment. Locate the jigsaw blade in the small cuts in the sides and make a cut across the ends where the hinges will sit.

8 Check the markings for the rest of the cut. A simple way to make curves is to draw round a cylinder. Cut along the lines on the long sides as far as the top surface.

7 Position the hinges with the hinge knuckle directly over the cut, mark the screw holes, and fit two screws per hinge to check alignment. Continue to fit the screws until they are all in place.

Fitting hinges

9 Before cutting across the top it is best to cut the wider slot that forms the handle. With a large drill, bore holes at the end of each slot.

10 Then cut this slot with the jigsaw. Now complete the final cut across the top, after which the two segments will hinge as shown.

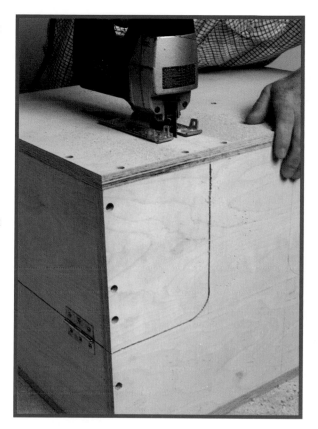

11 The illustration shows how the box opens at this stage. The hinged ends will not lie flat with the box ends, but will rest on the floor when the castors are applied.

CROSS REFERENCE	
Hinges	15
Sawing	13
Drilling	14

Plugging the holes

12 The main construction is now complete. If you wish to keep the box finish as natural plywood, it is a good idea to hide the heads of the screws by inserting timber plugs. Make sure that the heads of the screws are 6mm (¼ in) below the surface. Buy or make a dowel that will fit snugly into the hole in which the screw head sits, and cut this into short lengths that are long enough to allow you to trim flush later.

13 Apply glue to the holes and tap the dowels into place with a hammer. When the glue is dry, cut off any excess dowel length near the surface. Plane flush with the plywood surface. If you intend to paint the box, the screws can be recessed approximately 2mm (⅛in) and the holes filled with

decorating or car body filler, then filed or sanded flush.

14 At the moment the box has sharp corners, so soften these by putting a small round on all edges. Use a router with a special rounding cutter on the outside edges, and repeat this operation on the insides of the opening edges.

15 Sand all the flat surfaces with abrasive paper to give a good finish. Also sand the edges of the openings and hand slots smooth. Wrap abrasive paper round a flat block to sand panels, and round a shaped block to smooth curves and edges.

Finishing

16 The box is now ready to receive a finish. If it is to be left natural, apply a clear lacquer. If you plan to decorate the toybox, you now need to prepare it in the following way.

17 Give the inside of the box a coat of clear lacquer to keep it clean in use, but paint the outside with a coat of white primer/filler. Apply masking tape to all the edges, just short of the outside rounding – this will ensure a neat edge between the decoration and the inside of the box. Apply the masking tape as shown, ensuring that the outside edge is straight. Make sure of a crisp line at the corners by first masking over the corner and then trimming back to the precise line with a knife.

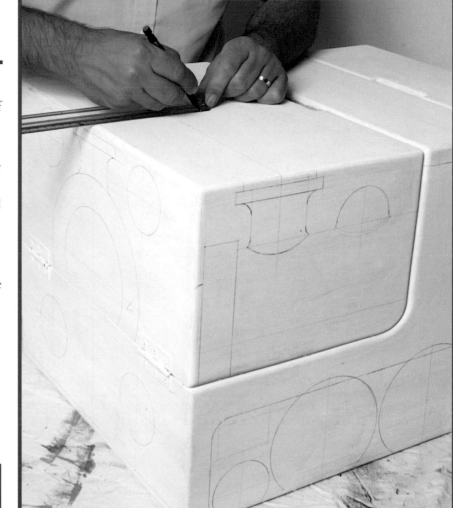

18 Apply primer/ filler to all the outside surfaces, making sure that the painting is complete right up to and over the masking tape on the inside edges, and that all the faces are covered.

◆ **Masking paintwork**

19 Now that the box has received its base coat, the illustrative decoration can be marked on the five outside faces. Using the illustration of the train as an example, measure the position of the main areas of colour and lay these out in pencil on the box. You may wish to design other forms of decoration, following the ideas suggested in the design spreads, or use ideas of your own.

CROSS REFERENCE	
Sanding	16
Painting	17

20 When marking out is complete, use a fine brush to paint the outline of the blocks of colour. For convenience, paint a straight edge with the help of a ruler. With this outline completed, it is relatively easy to paint in the mass of colour.

21 The pencil marks can be finished on all five sides, but it is convenient to paint one side at a time, with this surface flat. Mix up enough colour to complete the whole job and then paint each face.

22 Having achieved the overall effect with colours and outline shapes, apply details to each of the parts. The amount of detail can range from leaving the train with just its main colours, or painting close details such as rivets, handrails, name etc. Paint in this detail carefully on the faces with a fine brush.

23 When you are happy with the result and the paint is dry, apply a coat of clear lacquer to protect the decorative painting. Attach the castors to the base. When the box is fully open, small castors are lifted off the ground to prevent movement. If you use large castors the toybox will be fully mobile when open.

Toyboxes to Try

The original project was decorated as a train but this approach is easily adapted to other modes of transport. The castors are, of course, optional and give added mobility to the toybox. Remember to use small castors if you don't want the box to move while open.

Building Blocks The letters of the alphabet or numbers could be used to make the box look like a stack of building blocks, spelling out your child's name when the lid is open.

Ocean Liner Here the train has been turned into a ship on the sea by simply changing the drawings and the details painted on it. Instead of a liner it could be a luxury yacht or even a fishing boat.

Fire Engine
Here again the transport theme is used, but this time the box has been decorated to look like a fire engine, complete with a ladder and hose.

Alternative Openings
You can also try different proportional arrangements for opening the box, which are easy to achieve. Another variation is to cut the corners and hinge the flaps downwards, but this arrangement would not give the same play spaces as the original layout.

Dinosaur All children love dinosaurs and with this design you can have a friendly dinosaur or a fierce monster or dragon. The only limit is your child's imagination.

4

Classic Rocking Chair

This little rocking chair owes much to the tradition of chair making on both sides of the Atlantic. Its construction is influenced by the chair bodgers who made Windsor chairs in the beech woods of England, while much of the detail comes from the stick or rod chairs of communities such as the Shakers in America. The design will work well in either a natural timber finish, painted in

Shaker colours, or with applied decoration.

You can make the pieces of the chair from timber or from manufactured board using timber dowels or rods for the stick components. If you intend to paint or decorate the chair you could make all of the pieces, except the top back rail, from manufactured board such as MDF, particle board or plywood. Always use wooden dowels or rods for the sticks.

TOOLS

Hand	Power	Machine	Function
Plane	electric plane	surface planer	plane flat surface
Bow/coping saw	jigsaw	bandsaw	cut shapes
Tenon saw		dimension saw	cut straight
Spokeshave	belt sander	belt sander	smooth shapes
Brace/wheelbrace	electric drill	pillar drill	turn drill bits
Augur bits	twist drill	spade drill	drill large holes
Set of twist drills, 1mm to 6mm ($^1/_{32}$in to $^1/_4$in)			drill pilot and screw holes
Mortice and paring chisel			cut mortice, chisel ends of dowel
3 sash cramps			assembly
Screwdriver			insert screws
Pin hammer			insert panel pins
Pencil			mark out
Brush/mop			apply finish

CUTTING LIST

Part	No	Length	Width	Thickness
From solid wood				
Top back rail	1	330mm	70mm	40mm
		13in	2¾in	1½in
From solid wood or manufactured board if to be decorated				
Seat	1	350mm	320mm	20mm
		14in	12½in	¾in
Arms	2	260mm	60mm	20mm
		10½in	2⅜in	¾in

Part	No	Length	Width	Thickness
From solid wood or manufactured board if to be decorated				
Rockers	2	390mm	55mm	25mm
		15⅜in	2⅛in	1in
Back splat	1	235mm	80mm	6mm
		9¼in	3⅛in	¼in

Dowels	No	Total length	Shoulder length	Diameter
Front legs	2	240mm	215mm	25mm
		9½in	8½in	1in
Back legs	2	230mm	200mm	25mm
		9in	8in	1in
V/F back to front rails	2	250mm	215mm	20mm
		10in	8½in	¾in
V/F crossrail	1	285mm	260mm	15mm
		11¼in	10½in	⅝in
Back uprights	2	245mm	215mm	20mm
		9⅝in	8½in	¾in
Rear back supports	2	260mm	230mm	12mm
		10½in	9in	½in
Back dowels	2	240mm	215mm	9mm
		9½in	8½in	⅜in
Front arm supports	2	120mm	100mm	15mm
		4¾in	4in	⅝in
Intermediary arm supports	6	115mm	100mm	9mm
		4½in	4in	⅜in

Reduce the following dowels to these diameters at their ends.

	Diameter	Length of reduction
Front/back legs	15mm	15mm one end, 10mm the other
	⅝in	⅝in one end, 7/16in the other
V/F back to front rails	12mm	15mm each end
	½in	⅝in each end
V/F crossrail	12mm	12mm each end
	½in	½in each end
Back uprights	12mm	15mm one end, 10mm the other
	½in	⅝in one end, 7/16in the other
Front arm	9mm	10mm each end
	⅜in	7/16in each end

Plus: Glue, abrasive paper, sanding block, paper or card for templates, masking tape, screws, primer/sealer, paints, varnish, clear lacquer, wood stain, polish.

Plans and Elevations

Side elevation

Front elevation

50   200

100   300mm
1   6   12ins

Plan

2   8

Scale 1:10

Exploded view

Templates

Trace these templates to make the arms, back rail, rockers and seat of the chair. Use two templates joined together to form the back rail and seat.

⊞ Holes drilled from below

⊕ Holes drilled from above

Actual size

Back rail template

Armrest template

Rocker template

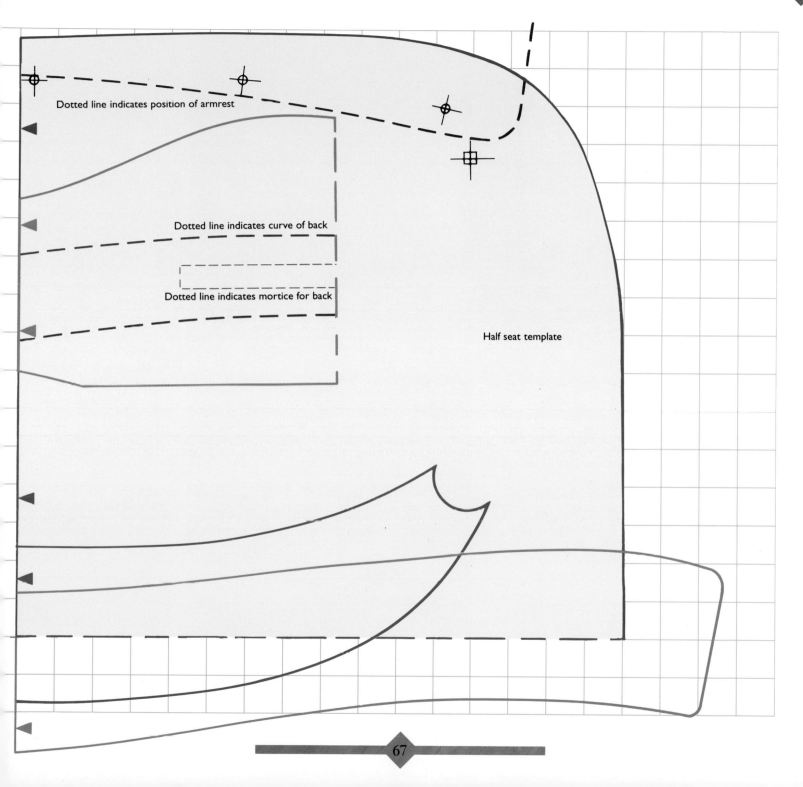

Dotted line indicates position of armrest

Dotted line indicates curve of back

Dotted line indicates mortice for back

Half seat template

1 To make the chair seat you may have to glue pieces together to obtain the correct width. Plane the edges so they are perfectly true, then glue the edges to be joined and cramp the boards together until the glue is dry. Remove the excess glue when wet with a damp rag, or scrape it off with a chisel blade when partly dry.

2 To mark out the shape of the seat, make a full-size paper template of the seat shape from the scale template provided. Position this onto the board and trace around it with a pencil. Use the template to mark the positions of the holes to be drilled for the dowels.

The holes under the seat are to accept the underframe, those on the top surface are for the back and arms. Use masking tape to hold the paper pattern in position on the top surface and use a centre punch and a pin hammer to mark the centre of the holes to be drilled.

3 Cut out the seat to the marked line; if you don't have a bandsaw use a hand power jigsaw or a hand coping saw. Once the seat is cut to shape, use the template to mark the exact positions of the holes to be drilled on the underside. Smooth the edges with a plane, spokeshave, rasp or file.

◤ **Using templates**

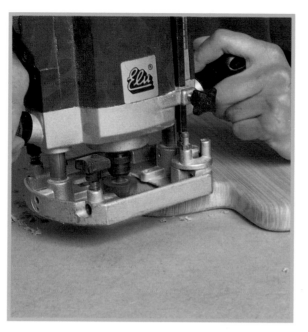

4 To remove the sharp edges you can use a router, if you have one, to put a radius around the seat both top and bottom. Sand the edge with abrasive paper.

5 Now drill the holes in the underside of the seat to accept the underframe. It is important to get the correct angle so make a jig that you can line up with the drill to give the correct angle outward and forward. Make jigs for both the front and back legs.

6 Drill the holes for both the back and the arms on the top of the seat in a similar way. Wrap a piece of masking tape around the drill bit as a guide to show that you have drilled to the correct depth.

7 The back splat slots into a mortice. You can cut this by boring a series of holes to remove the bulk of the waste. Then use a mortice chisel to clean out the hole to the required depth. Cramping a piece of straight timber with an angled side along the edge of the mortice helps to guide the chisel and make sure that the angle is correct. Put the seat aside and concentrate on the back.

CROSS REFERENCE	
Cramping	15
Using templates	9
Drilling	14
Joints	14

Making the back

10 When the block has been sawn from both faces, remove the waste by completing the cuts with a coping saw, or carefully on the bandsaw. Shape this cut rail with a spokeshave. A plane can be used on the convex side, or the whole rail may be shaped with a rasp and files. A belt sander is a useful tool for this job if you have one.

8 Cut the top back rail and shape it in two directions from a block of wood. Make a paper pattern to mark the shape on the plan and front. While the block is still square, cut the mortice for the back splat to sit in, in the same way as the mortice in the seat.

9 To shape the block, make cuts through the width of the timber from the top. At this stage do not cut right through to remove the waste, but leave small "fingers" to hold the waste in place, to make the next cut safer and easier. Turn the block on its side and again cut through the thickness; make sure that you leave some of the waste in place to support the rail.

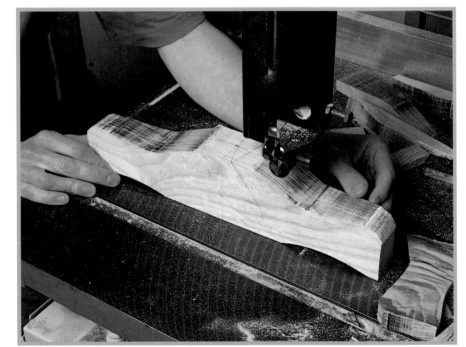

Finished back

11 Next, cut the dowels to the lengths on the cutting list. Some of the dowels will fit into the holes at their original diameter, but some will need to be reduced at their ends to fit into suitably sized holes. To do this mark the length that will fit into the hole and cut the shoulders on the dowel ends using a hand saw. Using a chisel, carefully pare into the dowel and reduce it to the desired diameter. Work carefully to avoid splitting the dowel.

12 When this rough cut is completed, true the end with a chisel. Use abrasive paper wrapped round a sanding block to remove the sharp corners.

Dowels

CROSS REFERENCE	
Chiselling	13
Sanding	16

The arms and rockers

14 Carefully mark out and drill the holes in the dowels that form the underframe and in the top back rail. Use a pillar drill (drill press), electric hand drill or wheelbrace to drill these holes. Placing a square or sliding level on the piece with its blade upright and in line with the drill bit will provide a guide for accurate drilling.

13 You will need to make two arms and two rockers. Cut these to shape in the same way as the back rail, making a template to mark out the shape first. Mark out and drill the holes in the underside of the arms to accept the dowels that support them.

15 Mark out on the rockers the position of the holes to take the legs, drill these holes, checking for depth and the correct angle.

Shaped rocker

16 With all the pieces cut to shape and the holes drilled, sand all the components with abrasive paper before starting to assemble.

Assembly

17 It is a good idea to put the chair together dry, without glue, to make sure the pieces fit, and allow for any adjustment. Try the back splat into the mortice in the seat and into the mortice in the top back rail. Use a chisel to finely pare the mortice to fit if necessary.

18 Take the four legs and the back-to-front rails of the underframe and fix them together, putting glue into the holes and cramping with sash cramps. Apply glue to each end of the crossrail and insert it to link these two assemblies. Fix the whole underframe into the underside of the seat and allow the glue to set.

19 Next, assemble the back components: top back rail, the back splat, the main side dowels, the back support dowels and the infill dowels. Assemble dry first to check that all is well, then glue the assembly in position at the back of the seat top.

Fixing the arms

20 Each arm is supported and fixed underneath by four upright dowels. The holes that the dowels fit into were drilled in the seat and underside of the arms earlier. Shape the back end of the arm to fit precisely onto the main back dowel. Use a rasp or a file to make a good fit.

21 Then fix the arm by gluing the upright dowels in position under the arms. Drill a pilot hole from the outside of the back upright dowel into the end of the arm. Screw through this back dowel and into the end of the arm to secure.

22 Finally, try fitting the rockers dry. Then glue and cramp in place and clean off the excess glue where necessary. Your chair is now ready to polish or paint as desired.

Finishing the chair

23 If you wish to decorate the chair with paint, first apply a white primer sealer. When this base coat is dry you can start to add colour and decoration. This chair was painted with a mixture of vinyl emulsion paint and artist's gouache. Paint the underside of the chair first then stand it up and paint the legs, seat, back and arms.

25 For a natural timber finish, use a clear lacquer. It is a good idea to apply lacquer, and stain if required, before the final assembly. First make sure that all the pieces fit and check that the lacquer does not fill the dowel holes or mortices. Put masking tape on the ends of the dowels and on the ends of the back splat so that the finish does not prevent the glue from adhering.

24 Decorations may be painted directly onto the chair or glued on. Select a picture, carefully cut round it, and apply glue to the reverse. Position the picture on the chair and rub down thoroughly. When the glue is dry the decoration may be protected with a coat of clear polyurethane varnish.

26 Although this is a classic design, it is easily transformed to suit your child and the natural and decorated versions look equally striking.

Really Rocking Chairs

We have one in natural wood and one painted with the frog theme. This piece lends itself to many interpretations and the following are examples you might find interesting. If you come up with some ideas of your own, so much the better.

The Royal The top back rail has been shaped to look like a crown with two wooden balls as orbs on the top of the back supports. The back slat has been widened and shaped to give a shield with a crest and the arms modified and thickened on the front to enable the carving of a lion's paw.

Pirate The top back rail has been enlarged to make way for the skull and crossbones and the back slat widened (thus removing the two thinner rails) so that a sail can be painted on this piece. The nautical theme can be continued with cord running between the rail and the rear back support. The larger dowels on the arms can be carved to represent rope and the rockers can be painted to look like the sea.

Humpty Dumpty This picks up on the theme shown in the matching chair and stool in project 8. The King and Humpty have been placed on top of the back supports, the slat widened to include a picture of Humpty falling off the wall, front rails detailed as soldiers similar to the other chair, and painting on the seat. This could look good in solid timber with painted illustrations.

Snakes and Ladders The back slat now flares into the top rail to give a picture of a smiling snake. Using thinner dowels, ladders can be made in the back and under the arms as shown and other snakes can be painted on the seat, legs and rockers.

Cutout Shapes and Colours The back slat is widened and slats put underneath the arms to allow for various cut out shapes and interesting colour effects.

5

Outdoor Playhouse

This sturdy and spacious playhouse is large-scale and is specifically designed for use in the garden. By reducing the scale younger children may use the playhouse inside the home. This design overcomes the problems of construction, and makes the door and window openings simple to make and easy to understand. All of the parts are cut from standard-sized manufactured board, in this case exterior grade plywood, which is used for both its structural and decorative properties. You will see from the drawings how to arrange the cutting of each component: base, four sides, veranda pieces and roof panels.

TOOLS

Hand	Power	Machine	Function
Panel saw	circular/jigsaw	dimension saw	cut to size
Padsaw	jigsaw		cut window and door openings
Hand drill	electric drill		drill screw holes
Twist drills			drill screw holes
Screwdriver			insert screws
Hammer			drive nails and pins
Brushes/mops			apply stain and finish

Part	No	Length	Width	Thickness
From exterior-quality plywood if for outdoors, in standard 2.4m x 1.2m (8ft x 4ft) sheets, 12mm (½in) thick				
Floor	1			
Long sides	2			
Gable ends	2	See drawings for cutting to final size		
Roof panels	2	See drawings for cutting to final size		

Part	No	Length	Width	Thickness
From offcuts of gable ends and roof panels				
Porch ends	2			
Capping pieces	2			

Part	No	Length	Width	Thickness
From preservative-treated sawn wood				
Bearers	9	1.2m	150mm	50mm
		4ft	6in	2in

Plus: Four hinges, screws, glue, nails, abrasive paper, bitumen felt, colour stain, clear varnish.

Plans and Elevations

Side elevation

Front elevation

Plan

150   600

300   900mm

3   18   36ins

6   24

Scale 1:30

Exploded view

Cutting the shapes

1 Mark out the ply for the two long and two short sides and follow the illustrations to see how to make the door and window openings. Making doors and windows is normally quite a complex woodworking operation, but this method is very simple and ensures that the openings will fit when finished. The illustrations detail the making of a glazed window, but you will use this basic principle to make the doors too. Start by marking out the position of a window on the ply. Mark the window panes and the surrounding frame.

2 Now drill a hole large enough to receive the blade of the jigsaw.

3 Cut out the areas that will be glazed. When you have cut out the required number of panes, prepare to partly cut along the line that will separate the frame and the wall.

4 You will need to drill an angled hole, so make a simple 30° jig to guide the drill.

5 Set the jigsaw to an angle of 30° when making the cut. It is essential that you only cut one side of the frame since the principles of construction behind this design depend on fitting the hinges in position at this stage. This method ensures that the window or door will fit its aperture exactly.

The hinges

6 The next stage is to fit the hinges. Drill a small pilot hole for the screws. It is important to place the hinge carefully on the line that you have cut with the jigsaw, so that the knuckle (the part around which the hinge opens) is exactly over the line and in line with the cut. Only insert a couple of screws to hold the hinge until you are sure that the correct position has been achieved.

7 Screw the two hinges in place over the cut line and then cut the other three sides of the frame with the jigsaw. Make sure that the cut is angled the same way on the three sides as the hinge side, and that the angle is from the outside towards the centre of the frame, so that the frame will "sit" into the wall from the outside where it is hinged. When the complete cut has been made all round the window or door, the frame will open easily.

8 A similar procedure is used for the door. Again, make sure to cut the hinged side first and fix the hinges before cutting the other three sides to create the door.

9 In this project the frames were coloured. To avoid the risk of accidentally staining adjacent parts, remove the window frame from the wall, noting carefully with letters or numbers which window goes where. Apply the finish, first by brush and then with a cloth.

Glazing the windows

10 This design uses rigid plastic sheet for the glazing. The plastic is safer than glass and is easily fitted using woodworking tools. First cut the plastic sheet to fit into position. Fix in place with screws, countersink the plastic sheet to receive the screw head, and then screw in place. It is better to do this before applying the sealing mastic between the plastic and frame.

12 Now put the plastic sheet back in place over the window frame.

11 Remove all the screws and apply mastic to the outside frame and to the mullions.

13 Make temporary marks to ensure that the sheet is relocated in exactly the same position, edge to edge, as it was when first screwed in place. Replace all the screws, then turn the sheet over and carefully remove any excess mastic that may have squeezed out.

14 Fit knobs to the windows and doors so they can be opened easily. There is a wide range of ready-made knobs available.

15 You will also need to cut out the openings as shown on the porch end to create the large, unglazed open "windows" of the veranda and the slatted railing effect beneath them.

Also cut the capping pieces, stain them to match the windows and, when dry, check for fit.

Assembling the house

16 Lay the base in position in the garden. If you used plywood, support it on timber bearers that have been treated against rot. These do not need to be planed, they can be sawn wood, and the ply should be fitted to them with screws. Where you locate the playhouse will depend on the ground conditions, but it is a good idea to ensure that the bearers do not sit directly on grass or earth. You can either remove any grass and topsoil and cover the area underneath with gravel, or place the bearers on brick or stone slabs with a damp-proof membrane in between for longer life.

17 The next step is to attach the rear end and one long side onto the base. Use locating pegs to position these pieces, or screw battens into the corners where the panels meet.

18 Fit the end with the door in position, then position the other long side to complete the sides. Now fit both the front cutout pieces of the veranda in place and secure the capping pieces on top of the railings.

19 Finish the assembly by attaching the two roof panels. Cut out the shaped barge boards and fix on the veranda end.

20 Finally, to make the roof waterproof, nail bitumen felt over the roof and eaves. The house is now ready for its new occupants to take up residence.

21 Add some garden furniture and perhaps a few home comforts and your children can play safely and cosily in this great hideaway for hours.

Let's Play House

The step-by-step illustrations show a playhouse for use in the garden, made in natural material with coloured stain. However, this design can also be made for internal use by reducing the scale. When adapting the house to other designs, add the appropriate items of furniture and decoration for authenticity.

Shop or Store With a little more effort, it would be possible to create a shop or stall by opening up one side and having a drop-down counter. You can leave the roof as it is or change its profile. Adapt the door as necessary and then decorate the whole piece with awnings and appropriate shop signs.

Hospital Using a similar arrangement as the original, the basic playhouse could be converted easily with appropriate windows, doors and graphics in the form of signs and symbols showing the nature of the building. This way the building could be anything from a disco to a police station.

Windows These are just two examples of the infinite variety of windows the playhouse can have. Remember to change the doors to suit any design you choose.

Chimneys You could add a chimney or a skylight to the roof of the house, but remember that this could cause problems outdoors.

Rooftops In addition to a chimney, you can also paint the roof to make it look like different materials such as tiles, slates or even thatch.

Garage This novel approach is very simple: just change the doors so that they are almost the width of the house and your child has a perfect garage for his or her pedal cars and bicycles.

Added Decorations Why not just simply liven up the original playhouse by adding some flowers, bushes or even small trees around the veranda area.

6

Aztec Pyramid Storage Unit

This piece of furniture is a different and unusual approach to a child's storage unit since, as well as storing objects, the shape allows a child to climb the structure to look in the "surprise" box on the top. For younger children it would be advisable to provide handles and possibly a support rail. The decoration is based on an Aztec theme, but many different approaches could be considered.

The construction is fairly simple, as the unit is built from a set of similar but different-sized boxes, each of which contains a drawer. These drawers are placed one on top of the other, but offset to one side and towards the back.

The unit is made from manufactured board, either MDF or particle board, and basically consists of the following components: three "boxes" which hold the drawers: three drawers to fit; one box on top with a hinged lid, and a plinth to raise the bottom drawer off the floor.

TOOLS

Hand	Power	Machine	Function
Panel saw	circular saw	dimension saw/ radial arm saw	cut to size/make joints
Shoulder and rebate plane	router		make joints
Plane			smooth edges
Hand drill/wheelbrace	electric drill		drill screw holes
Brace	electric drill	pillar drill	turn drill bits
Augur or expansion bits for brace or spade bits/forstner bits			drill handle holes
Screwdriver			insert screws
Brushes/sponges			apply finish
Marker/felt-tip pen			draw shapes

CUTTING LIST

Part	No	Length	Width	Thickness
From manufactured board (MDF)				
Drawer holders				
Bottom unit	2	600mm	600mm	12mm
top/bottom		24in	24in	½in
Sides/back	3	600mm	150mm	12mm
		24in	6in	½in
Middle unit	2	475mm	475mm	12mm
top/bottom		18¾in	18¾in	½in
Sides/back	3	475mm	150mm	12mm
		18¾in	6in	½in
Top unit	2	350mm	350mm	12mm
top/bottom		14in	14in	½in
Sides-back	3	350mm	150mm	12mm
		14in	6in	½in
Surprise box sides	4	230mm	200mm	12mm
		9in	8in	½in
Base	1	130mm	230mm	12mm
		9in	9in	½in
Top, halved diagonally	1	230mm	230mm	12mm
		9in	9in	½in
Bottom drawer base	1	570mm	570mm	12mm
		22½in	22½in	½in
back/front	2	580mm	125mm	12mm
		23in	5in	½in
sides	2	570mm	125mm	12mm
		22½in	5in	½in
Middle drawer base	1	430mm	430mm	12mm
		17in	17in	½in
back/front	2	440mm	125mm	12mm
		17½in	5in	½in
sides	2	430mm	125mm	12mm
		17in	5in	½in
Top drawer base	1	320mm	320mm	12mm
		12½in	12½in	½in
back/front	2	330mm	125mm	12mm
		13in	5in	½in
sides	2	320mm	125mm	12mm
		12½in	5in	½in
From solid wood				
Plinth	4	580mm	50mm	30mm
		23in	2in	1¼in

Plus: Piano hinge, glue, screws, filler, nails/pins, abrasive paper, primer/sealer, paints.

Plans and Elevations

Side elevation

Front elevation

Plan

50   200

100   300mm
1   6   12ins

2   8   Scale 1:10

Exploded views

The drawer holders

1 First make the "boxes" or drawer holders. These are all five-sided boxes, square on plan, the open side of which will accept the drawer. They are all made in the same way, differing only in size.

2 Cut the top and bottom of each drawer holder to size. Having cut one corner precisely square, the two parts can be made to the precise size by cramping a stop to the fence and then cutting sides three and four. A radial arm or pull over saw is used here but a table saw will do; or they can be cut carefully by hand.

3 Now cut the back and two sides to width and just over length. In order to locate the sides accurately the back has a lap worked at the ends. Therefore this will be the same length as the top/bottom. The sides are slightly shorter to accept this lap. Cut the overall lengths using the same stop positions as for the top. Then cut the laps on the back component by inserting a spacer equal to the thickness of the side material.

4 Remember to adjust the depth so that a cut is made halfway through the thickness only. The excess outside the shoulder line can now be removed to the same depth by making several cuts. Now cut the two sides to length. They will be shorter than the top by the thickness of the lap joint.

5 The top and bottom can be prepared ready for assembly. Mark the positions of the screw holes, drill pilot holes to receive the screws and then countersink these to accept the screw head. To help the drawers run smooth, you can attach some iron-on drawer runner tape along the sides where they meet the bottom.

Drawer holder

6 Locate the top on the three sides, having first fixed the lap joint on the back corners. It is wise to insert the screws without gluing the joint so that you can check that everything is square. Remember that the front of this box will accept the drawer and the inside space between the two sides needs to be exactly parallel, so cut a spare piece to a length that is exactly the distance between the lap shoulders and place this at the front opening to ensure the correct dimension and thus make the sides parallel.

7 Follow the same procedure with the bottom and, if all is well, remove the screws, apply glue and reassemble. When the glue is dry, fill all the screw heads and finally shave the box sides with a plane to make them flat and smooth. Repeat the procedure with the other two drawer holders.

The surprise box

8 Now make the "carcase" of the surprise box. It is made in a similar way to the other boxes, but the open face is the top rather than one of the sides. When assembly is complete, hold the box in the vice and smooth the outside surfaces.

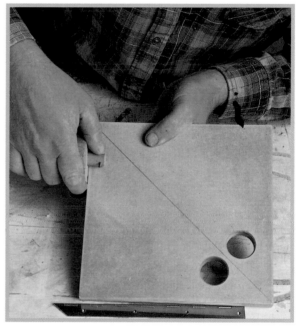

9 Before assembling the complete unit, make and fit the top flaps to this box. Cut the two triangles to size and drill a hole in a corner of each to act as handles. Set the marking gauge to the piano hinge, from one edge to the centre of the knuckle.

10 Gauge the two sides where you will fit the hinge. Reset the gauge to the thickness of the closed hinge and gauge the thickness.

11 Make a shallow rebate on these sides and position the hinge in the rebate so that the closed hinge is level with the inside surface.

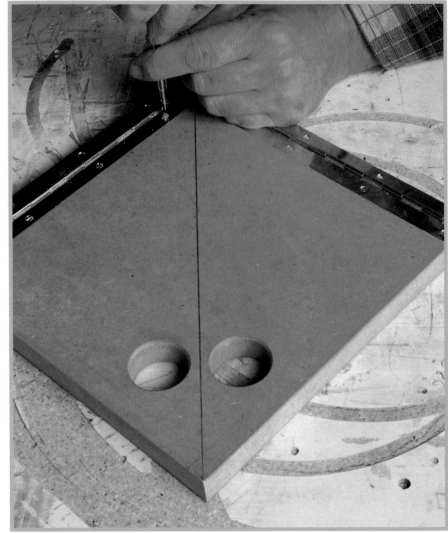

12 Lay the triangular flaps in place and mark the position of the hinges, and then the position of the screw holes.

13 Now fit the flaps in position and check that they open and close correctly.

14 Then remove the flaps, true up the closing edge and apply a sealing coat to that edge. The three drawer boxes and the surprise box are now ready for assembly.

Fitted flaps

Drawer making and assembly

15 Apply the plinth to the bottom of the lower drawer holder. This is made from four lengths, mitred at the corners and screwed and glued into position, approximately 30mm (1¼in) from the outside edge. Mark the position of the next drawer holder and insert two screws at the open drawer face to hold its position. Do not glue this assembly yet, as it is easier to apply a finish to the separate components.

16 Continue positioning all the drawer holders and the surprise box.

17 Now make the drawers to fit the drawer holders – prepare a base and four sides. The drawers are made in a similar way to the drawer holders, but the base sits in rebates in the sides. Use a router to make rebates so that the sides can be fitted to the drawer bottom in a similar way to the drawers of the circus wardrobe.

Finished drawer

19 When the three drawers are complete, fit them into the unit. Drill a hole to act as a pull to open each drawer.

18 Cut a rebate on the ends of the front and back, but not on the ends of the sides, so that a lap joint is formed on each of the four corners, with the front and back overlapping the sides. Working a chamfer onto the back edges will help ease the fit in the holders. Assembling the sides around the base will help keep the drawer square. Drill holes for screws into the lap joint through the sides, or nail together with pins. Countersink the screws or punch the nail heads in and fill with filler, then smooth.

Decorating

20 Now disassemble the unit prior to decorating. Mask the top of each drawer holder just inside the position of the one on top. Apply a coat of primer/filler on all components, including the fronts of the drawers. The final colours and decorative motifs can now be applied.

21 Add texture to the paint surface using a sponge and mix some paint to finish the details.

22 When the textured base coat has dried, apply the decorative motifs. They can be painted on, but here we used permanent markers to draw the patterns. First, mark out using tracing paper to transfer the pattern; the straight lines can be drawn in with a ruler.

24 This highly original chest of drawers is very strong and well-made, with plenty of storage space and the added attraction of the "secret" box for your child's special possessions.

23 The curves and other patterns are then drawn in by hand. When the decoration is finished, seal the whole piece with clear lacquer to protect it.

The Storage Depot

As mentioned earlier in the project, this is an extremely strong unit which will easily cope with children clambering on it. For very small children, however, add some hand rails at the corners as an extra safety measure. Your children will enjoy painting and decorating the drawers in their own designs.

Native Tent Following the theme of ancient civilizations, create a Native American variation with poles fixed to the corners of the drawers and canvas sides added to suggest a tepee or wigwam, decorated with suitable motifs.

Building Blocks Another approach is to paint the cabinets as coloured blocks with letters on them, like a tower of building bricks. This design could then be matched with the toybox and with the shelving unit shown later in the book. Experiment with the many combinations of letters, numbers and colours.

Ancient Egypt Similar to the original Aztec theme, this variation is inspired by Egyptian figures and hieroglyphics. This design is great fun, as your child can create his or her personal rebus puzzle, perhaps leading to the secret of the surprise box at the top – a little like Indiana Jones on his adventures.

Drawer Variants There are, of course, alternative drawer arrangements. If you have enough space, the drawers can be made to open from each of the four sides, with the secret compartment having a lift-off lid and the bottom two drawers split. Having decided on a theme, you could also paint each face the same, as dummy drawers.

7

Shapely Shelves

This shelving system is based on a series of geometric solids; the one illustrated was made to suit smaller children. It is possible, however, to increase the size for older children simply by altering the ratio of the measurements. The system is made in component form so you will have to make the support poles/bases, the shelves and a series of geometric solids: rectangles, cubes, cylinders, pyramids, cones, spheres etc. The two support poles are made from timber rods, such as readily available large dowels or broomsticks, while the bases are made from manufactured board. The shelves can also be made from manufactured board or, as in this example, from solid timber. Make the shapes by gluing together joinery grade softwood to sizes large enough from which to cut the required components. This practical system should be as colourful as possible.

TOOLS

Hand	Power	Machine	Function
4 or 6 sash cramps			hold glued blocks
Handsaw	circular/jigsaw	radial arm saw/ dimension saw	cut softwood to length/make joints
Plane			smooth surfaces
Hand drill and brace	electric drill	pillar drill	drill for base holes
Auger bits, expansion bit, spade and forstner bits			drill holes
Brushes			apply finish

CUTTING LIST

Part	No	Length	Width	Thickness
From 12mm (½in) MDF				
Base sides	8	300mm	100mm	12mm
		12in	4in	½in
Base tops	2	300mm	300mm	12mm
		12in	12in	½in
From timber rod or dowel				
Support poles	2	900mm	30mm diam.	
		35in	1¼in diam.	
From solid wood				
Shelves	4	930mm	200mm	25mm
		36½in	8in	1in

Solids

From 7m x 225mm x 50mm (23ft x 9in x 2in) joinery softwood.

	Dimensions after shaping	Starting length	Cut into (number of pieces)/length
Top pyramid	200 x 200 x 200mm	800mm	(4 pieces)/200mm
	8 x 8 x 8in	31½in	(4)/8in
Top sphere	215mm diam.	800mm	(4)/200mm
	8½in diam.	31½in	(4)/8in
2 top cubes	150 x 150 x 150mm	2 pieces	(3)/150mm
	6 x 6 x 6in	of 450mm	(3)/6in
		2 x 17¾in	
Rectangle	250 x 200 x 150mm	750mm	(3)/250mm
	10 x 8 x 6in	29½in	(3)/10in
Cylinder	200mm diam. x 150mm	600mm	(3)/200mm
	8in diam. x 6in	24in	(3)/8in
Truncated pyramid	150 x 150 x 100mm	300mm	(2)/150mm
	6 x 6 x 4in	12in	(2)/6in
Small cube	100 x 100 x 100mm	200mm	(2)/100mm
	4 x 4 x 4in	8in	(2)/4in
Octagon	180 x 180 x 150mm	600mm	(3)/200mm
	7 x 7 x 6in	24in	(3)/8in
Rectangle	200 x 200 x 150mm	600mm	(3)/200mm
	8 x 8 x 6in	24in	(3)/8in
Sphere	170mm diam. x 150mm	545mm	(3)/180mm
	6¾in diam. x 6in	21½in	(3)/7in
Cone	200mm diam. x 150mm	600mm	(3)/200mm
	8in diam. x 6in	24in	8in

Plus: Glue, pins, abrasive paper, filler, primer/sealer, paints, clear varnish.

Plans and Elevations

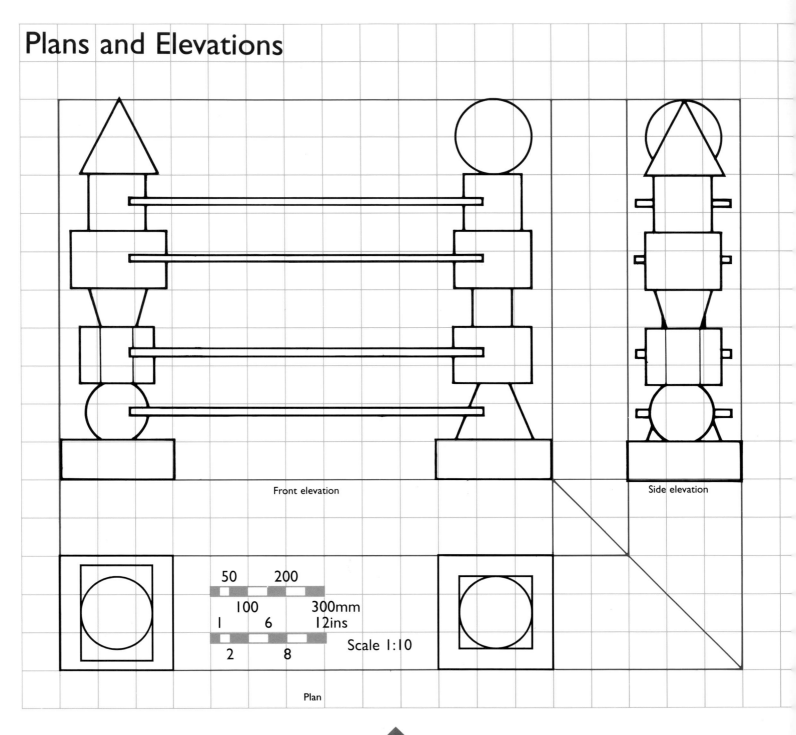

Front elevation

Side elevation

50   200

100   300mm

1   6   12ins

Scale 1:10

2   8

Plan

Exploded view

The shelves

1 Make the first set of components – the two support poles and bases. Cut some manufactured board to make the top and four sides of a five-sided box; construct these using a similar method to that used to make the drawer holders shown in the storage unit. Mark the centre of the top face and drill a hole that will accept the pole. Using some of the softwood offcuts, glue a stack of approximately 150mm (6in) over the hole and, when the glue is dry, continue drilling the hole to a predetermined depth, making sure that it is precisely vertical. Then glue the support pole in place in the hole and sand ready for finishing.

2 Now make the shelves. Prepare the timber to the correct size – length, width and thickness. Plane and sand smooth to ensure a good surface. Since some of the corners of the shelves project from the solids, it is advisable to round the corners. Use a washer or other appropriately sized disc and mark the round.

3 Saw off the corner before rounding with a plane, chisel or rasp. After a final sanding the shelves are ready for finishing.

Support poles and bases

4 Next make the
   shapes. These were
made by gluing together
planks of timber as it is
unlikely that you will
find solid timber of a
large enough size and, if
you did, you could not
be sure if it was dry or
stable enough. By
laminating the blocks,
you can be sure of the
moisture content and
gain greater stability. Cut
the planks into standard
lengths from which the
shapes can be cut,
allowing at least 70mm
(2¾in) of waste on the
end for final trimming.
Apply glue to the faces to
be joined. To prevent
these lengths from
slipping out of place
when you apply the
cramps, partially insert a
nail as a location.

5 Apply enough
   cramps to give the
required pressure and
leave the glue to dry.

CROSS REFERENCE	
Sawing	12
Adhesives	15
Planing	13
Cramping	15

6 When the glue has cured, plane the long-grain faces square and saw the end-grain faces square. It is unsafe to try to make this cut in one pass, and it is unlikely that most woodworkers would have a circular saw large enough. So, make a cut one-third deep on the four faces, using a fence to guide the work. Then finish the cut with a handsaw. Make enough of these blocks to complete the required number of shapes.

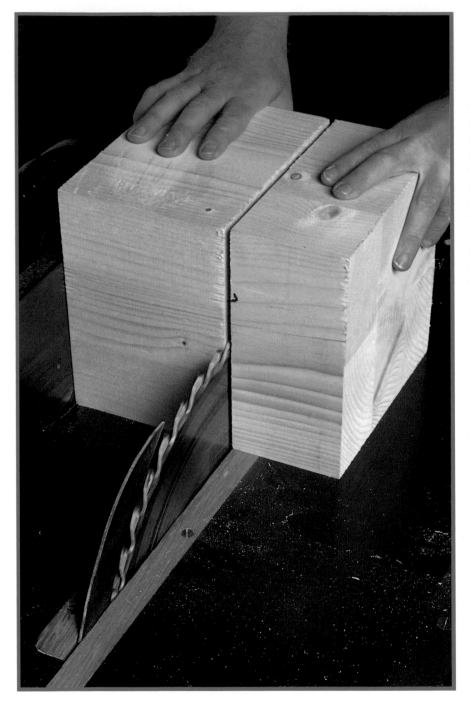

7 Cut the shapes to their overall sizes and proceed to mark, cut and shape each piece. Before starting the final shaping, it is wise to cut the slots that will receive the shelves. It is safer to make these cuts while the blocks are square. Make two parallel sawcuts that will give a slot of the required width. *Note:* The guard has been removed for photographic clarity, but this is not recommended in general practice. Remove the waste with a chisel of a smaller or equivalent width.

Final shaping

8 Some of the geometric solids are simple adaptations of a rectangular block; some need further elaborate cutting and shaping. The basic block is rectangular, and from this a cube can easily be cut. It is simple to mark out an octagon on a cube and then cut off and plane the four new faces.

9 Mark the centre on all the shapes and drill a hole to accept the support pole.

Shaped blocks

10 A pyramid can be made in a similar way to the truncated solid. Since the top comes to a point, once the first cut is made it is safer to nail the waste offcut back in place so that the next side can be cut safely. Keep your hands away from the saw blade.

11 Other shapes may need to be turned but the cylinder can be made either way. Mark the centre and use a compass or trammel to mark the circumference.

12 It is possible to cut this cylinder on a bandsaw and then plane and sand the edges smooth or, having sawn off most of the waste, to place the block in a lathe and turn it to a cylinder.

13 To make a sphere or cone mark the centre and cut as for a cylinder, but then turn the required shape. The cone is simply a matter of turning a straight line from the cylindrical base to its tip. The sphere needs to be turned, so carefully shape the block from a cylinder to the final shape in stages. It is a good idea to make a cardboard template of the sphere which can be used to check the progress of the turning. Gradually round the ends of the block to create a sphere.

CROSS REFERENCE	
Marking shapes	9
Sawing	13
Woodturning	12

Finishing

14 All the shapes will need filling (especially the end grain) and sanding in preparation for finishing. Apply a primer/filler coat to all the components to be coloured and decorated (the shapes and the base). Apply clear or coloured lacquer to the shelves and leave the support posts unfinished.

15 When the primer/filler is dry, paint and decorate. Aerosol spray paints will produce a good finish if you follow the instructions on the can. Mount each solid on a pole to spray different colours. Finally, assemble the stacks of solids onto the poles, position the shelves and the system is ready to use.

16 This very colourful and practical unit has the added advantage of being completely adjustable. You and your children will have great fun rearranging the supporting blocks.

Stacks of Shelves

T he initial project here uses wooden blocks cut to the various platonic solids and painted. Once you have made the starting blocks, try turning them to different shapes from those used in the photographs, making sure that the slots for the shelves remain lined up.

Building Blocks Here the original blocks are kept the same shape as in the project, but letters have been painted on them. You can, of course, use numbers or, as shown in the alternative examples for the toybox, spell out your child's name. Don't forget that the shelves are adjustable and that the blocks can be repositioned to spell different words.

The Chess Set Here the shapes are a little more complex but a theme based on these chess pieces works very well. Why not try the carving technique shown later for making the animal bed project for the horse's head of the chess knight. For something less ambitious, you could model the blocks on draughts counters, similar to those shown below in the natural-look shelves.

The Natural Look If a reasonable match of the timber grain is achieved, the shapes can be left natural and simply varnished. Again, though, don't forget that you can vary the shapes of the blocks and the number of shelves.

Beach Balls This fun and highly colourful variation uses beach balls and buckets in a balancing act. It could even follow on from the circus theme used in other projects.

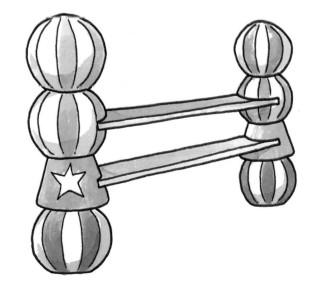

Humpty Dumpty Stool and Chair

These pieces make an interesting set using the theme of Humpty Dumpty in an original way. The techniques include turning to produce the legs and rails, and to apply the nursery rhyme decorative shaping. The stool is very simple and, if you are not used to turning, try this first. The chair, like the stool, is made with a solid timber seat. Most of the other components are cylindrical, many with turned decoration These pieces are beautifully finished and made to last.

TOOLS

Hand	Power	Machine	Function
Lathe gouges and chisels		lathe	turn components
Hand/coping saw	jigsaw	bandsaw	cut components
Plane	electric plane	surfacer/thicknesser	plane seats
Sash cramps			assembly
Band/web cramps			assembly
Hand drill	electric drill	pillar drill	drill holes
Assorted twist drills, auger, spade or forstner bits			drill holes
Calipers			check turning diameter
Spokeshaves	router		apply small rounds
Screwdriver			insert screws
Hammer			apply wedges
Chisel			trim wedges
Brushes/mops	spray gun		apply finish

CUTTING LIST

Part	No	Length	Width	Thickness
From solid wood				
Stool seat	1	230mm diam.		25mm
		9in diam.		1in
Stool legs	4	230mm		45mm diam.
		9in		1¾in diam.
Chair seat	1	295mm	280mm	20mm
			taper to 230mm	
		11¾in	11in	¾in
			taper to 9in	
Back legs	2	665mm		35mm diam.
		26¼in		1⅜in diam.
Front legs	2	320mm		35mm diam.
		12½in		1⅜in diam.
Top back rail	1	230mm	45mm	20mm
		9in	1¾in	¾in
Lower back rails	2	230mm		25mm diam.
		9in		1in diam.
Lower front to back rails	4	245mm		15mm diam.
		9⅝in		⅝in diam.
Lower crossrails	2	230mm		25mm diam.
				(taper to 15mm)
		9in		1in diam.
				(taper to ⅝in)
Soldier back splats	3	170mm		30mm diam.
		6¾in		1¼in diam.

Plus: Glue, clear lacquer, paints, abrasive paper, card/plywood for templates.

Plans and Elevations

Side elevation

Front elevation

Plan

50   200

100   300mm

1   6   12ins

2   8

Scale 1:10

Templates

Exploded view

These are full-size templates for shaping the King (left of dotted line) and Humpty (right) at the top of the back legs of the chair. Trace round the outlines to produce a "negative" of each profile.

Plans and Elevations

Side elevation

Front elevation

Plan

Exploded view

25   100
50   150mm
    3   6ins
1   4   Scale 1:5

Templates

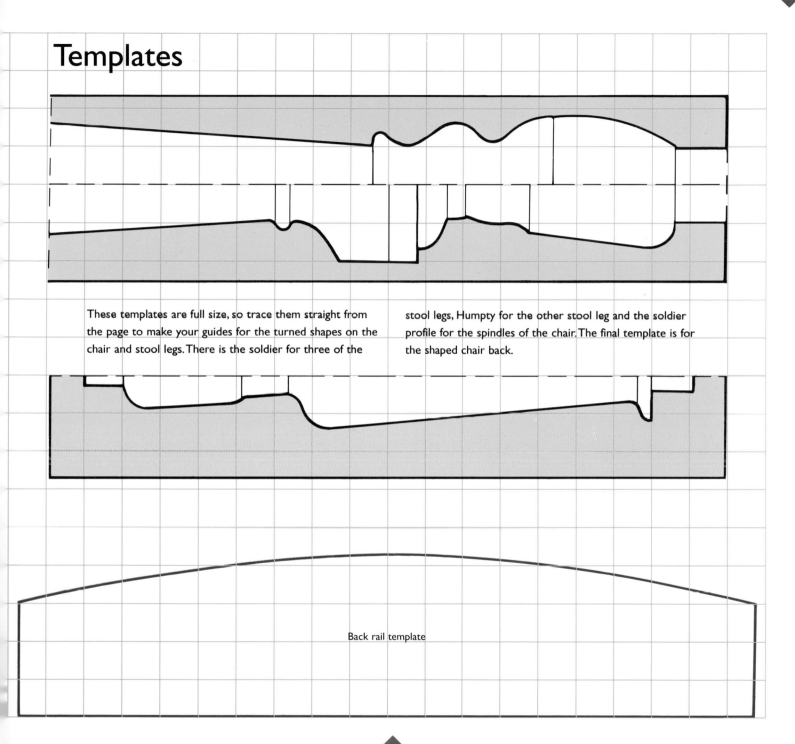

These templates are full size, so trace them straight from the page to make your guides for the turned shapes on the chair and stool legs. There is the soldier for three of the stool legs, Humpty for the other stool leg and the soldier profile for the spindles of the chair. The final template is for the shaped chair back.

Back rail template

The stool seat

1 The seat is made from natural timber which may need to be glued from smaller pieces if the width is not available. This procedure is illustrated in the rocking chair project (page 68).

Mark the circle for the seat and cut it out with a bowsaw, jigsaw or bandsaw. You can use a jigsaw or router like a compass to make this cut.

2 It is good practice to make a small round on the edges of the disc and this can be achieved by using a router with a suitable cutter. These processes can, of course, be carried out using hand tools if you do not have machines. A spokeshave will enable you to smooth the cut edge and to apply the round.

3 Now mark the positions for the four legs using a compass or a set of dividers. Mark the radius of the circle on which the leg centres will lie and mark the four points.

Making the stool legs

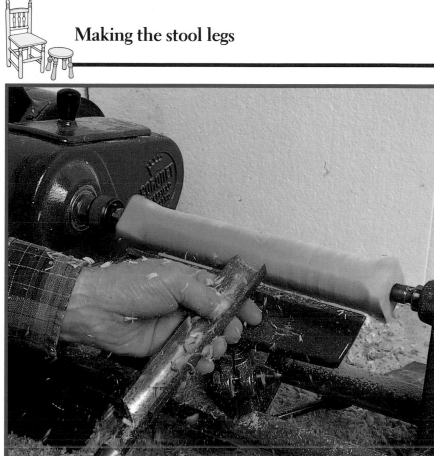

4 The legs splay outwards and to achieve this you will need to drill the holes at an angle. Make a jig that will hold the seat at the correct angle to the vertical pillar drill and drill the four holes.

5 Now make the four legs. This is where you will use the lathe. Cut the wood to be turned slightly over final length, and mark the centres of the timber at each end. Marks from the four corners giving diagonal lines will achieve an exact centre.

Fit the timber into the lathe; the left-hand end is the driving end, from motor to timber, and the other end simply runs free. Now take the turning gouge or chisel and make careful cuts to remove the corners of the wood. Continue turning until the leg is round.

CROSS REFERENCE	
Cutting curves	36
Drilling jigs	14
Wood turning	12

6 During the process of turning, check that you are nearing the required diameter. You can use calipers set to the required measurement for this when the lathe has stopped.

7 Having turned the cylindrical leg, turn the shapes for the decoration. The first stage is to do some shaping by eye, in this case for the "Humpty" shape. Make sure when turning the ends of the legs that they will fit exactly into the holes that you have drilled in the seat.

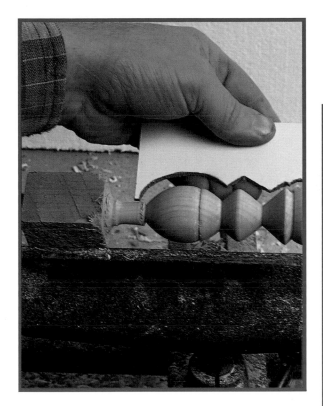

8 Now, using the appropriate template, check that the shaping is correct. Use the calipers to check the diameter of the ends. Continue to shape the three other "soldier" legs and sand these components as shown in step 11. You can then paint the four legs following the sequence on page 136 before assembly.

9 The legs can now be fitted to the seat. Apply glue to the ends of the legs and fit into the holes. Either drill the holes so that they do not come through the top, or drill through and wedge the legs in place. If you decide on the latter you will have a stronger joint. Remember to make a sawcut in the end of the legs and hammer in wedges from the top.

This process is shown in the chair sequence. Chisel the wedges flat and smooth with abrasive paper (see step 23).

CROSS REFERENCE	
Wood turning	12
Using templates	9
Joints	14

Making the chair

10 Make the turned components in the same way as you did for the stool, shaping by eye and then using a template to make sure of the exact shape required. This is the "soldier" spindle for the back but you will also need to shape the "King" and "Humpty" for the back legs. Turn the ends of each decoration to the correct size to fit in the crossrails, checking again with calipers.

11 Finally, check that you have the shape you require and sand the turned components. In order to work safely, place the abrasive paper behind the work, holding it from the underneath by its edge. Then use your other hand simply to guide the abrasive paper from the back onto the revolving work. Never try to grip – just press lightly on the sheet of abrasive which is held safely in your other hand, well below the turning wood.

12 Check that you have made all the parts. There should be: 1 back frame comprising: 2 back legs with Humpty and the King turned at the top, 1 rectangular top rail, 3 turned soldier spindles and 1 turned crossrail; another turned crossrail at the bottom under the seat; 2 front legs with some turning just under the seat; 2 sets of 2 rails from the back legs to the front legs; 1 crossrail between the front legs; 1 solid seat.

Drilling the holes

13 Drill holes in the front and back legs to receive the turned crossrails. Make a jig so that the turned pieces fit securely and are held safely in place while you drill the holes.

14 When drilling the back legs, having first drilled the rails that go across to make the back frame, you will then need to drill holes for the rails that go from back to front, making sure that they are at the correct angle to those you have already drilled. You need to adapt your jig in this case so that you can put a temporary dowel in the holes that you have drilled, then align the work with the drill so that the second holes are at the correct angle. When this drilling is done, try assembling the chair dry, making sure all parts fit and make any adjustments as necessary.

CROSS REFERENCE

Abrasives	16
Drilling	14

Painting

15 Before assembling the chair, apply the finish to the three soldiers in the back splat using the following painting sequence: tunic; trousers; bearskin; feet; white belt and the facial features. These are much easier to paint when they are separate pieces than when assembled.

16 The two decorative turnings at the top of the back legs – Humpty and the King – can be painted before or after assembly.

Assembly

17 It is customary in chair making to assemble the back frame first. Make the feature comprising the top back rail, three turned soldiers and bottom turned rail. Apply glue to the holes and assemble these parts.

18 Now assemble the complete back using sash cramps, making sure that the whole frame is square.

19 Assemble the two front legs and the front crossrail together and glue in position at the seat front. As before, hold the assembly in sash cramps.

CROSS REFERENCE	
Painting	17
Joints	14
Cramping	15

20 In order to fix the front legs to the seat, the legs project through the seat and are wedged in place. At this stage hammer in wedges.

21 When the glue for this assembly has dried, fix the seat and front-to-back rails in position, having first applied glue. This assembly can now be cramped using band or web cramps.

22 The seat sits in a small groove in the back legs; reinforce this joint by screwing through from the outside of the back leg into the seat. Recess the screw into the leg, and insert a plug to hide it.

23 Now the chair is assembled, other general finishing can be carried out. Earlier we glued wedges when assembling the front legs to the seat. Chisel them flat, then smooth with abrasive paper. Finally, check the chair all over and apply the final finish. Wipe with matt varnish and then apply wax-polish. The same finish can be applied to the stool.

Sitting Pretty

Although the original project was made using the theme of Humpty Dumpty, other nursery rhymes or stories would work just as well, as shown by these examples. Although these illustrations show the adaptations on the chair, they can also apply to the matching stool.

Characters Here the same principle as in the original project is used, but with some of the characters from *Alice in Wonderland*. As an example there is Alice, the Queen, the Cheshire Cat and the Mad Hatter. A variation on the soldier is used in the back assembly.

Cutouts and Colours As with the crib, you can also use cutouts – numbers and letters in bold colours. This approach also works well with geometric shapes similar to those in the shelving system. Paint your child's name on the shaped blocks on the back. Another colourful option is the balancing balls alternative, also shown for the shelving system.

Planets This is a simple but effective addition to the spacecraft theme on the following page. Turn the top of the leg to form a sphere and then paint it to look like Earth or one of the other planets.

Spacecraft This design could also use a theme such as spacecraft, and many items of space hardware can be turned to make parts of the chair and stool. Here we have rockets, lunar modules and even aliens. Don't forget to add your child's favourite planet, as shown on the previous page, perhaps to the legs of the stool.

Alternative Shapes If you prefer to keep it simple, the chair will also work well with different shapes and styles for the back. These are all in the natural finish, giving the piece a sophisticated look.

Combinations This illustration shows a combination of cutout shapes, colours and the turned characters from *Alice in Wonderland* used to good effect.

9

Wild Animal Bed

The design of this piece is an interesting and original departure from a bed. It is basically composed of two carvings of an animal, in this case a leopard. The two cats stand either side of the bed with a base board between them to support the mattress. The headboard is held between the two tails. You could, of course, adapt this design and choose a different four-legged animal of approximately the same proportions, but an elephant probably would not be suitable.

The construction of this bed is similar to the shelving system (see page 110) but on a larger scale. It is made from gluing joinery softwood together to form the outline of the timber block from which the detail is then carved.

TOOLS

Hand	Power	Machine	Function
Sash cramps/G-cramps			assembly
Brace/wheelbrace and drill bits	electric drill	pillar drill	drill dowel holes
Panel and coping saws	jigsaw	bandsaw	cut lengths and shapes
Carving gouges	wood grinder		carving
Carving mallet	router		grooving
Brushes			finish and decoration
Blow lamp			decoration

CUTTING LIST

Part	No	Length	Width	Thickness
From 75mm (3in) sawn joinery softwood				
Main spine	2	2200mm	150mm	70mm
		7ft 2½in	6in	2¾in
Legs	8	610mm	115mm	70mm
		24in	4½in	2¾in
Heads	2	430mm	230mm	70mm
		17in	9in	2¾in
Tails	4	790mm	130mm	70mm
		2ft 7in	5in	2¾in

Use offcuts for thickening at shoulder, flanks and legs.

From plywood

Headboard	1	800mm	610mm	9mm
		2ft 7½in	2ft	⅜in
Headboard curved battens	2	595mm	50mm	15mm
		23⅜in	2in	⅝in
Perforated base	1	1940mm	915mm	18mm
		6ft 4½in	3ft	¾in
Crossrails	3	to come		

Plus: Glue, abrasive paper, dowels, sealer, paints.

Plans and Elevations

Side elevation

Front elevation

Plan

150	600	
300		900mm
3	18	36ins
6	24	

Scale 1:30

Exploded views

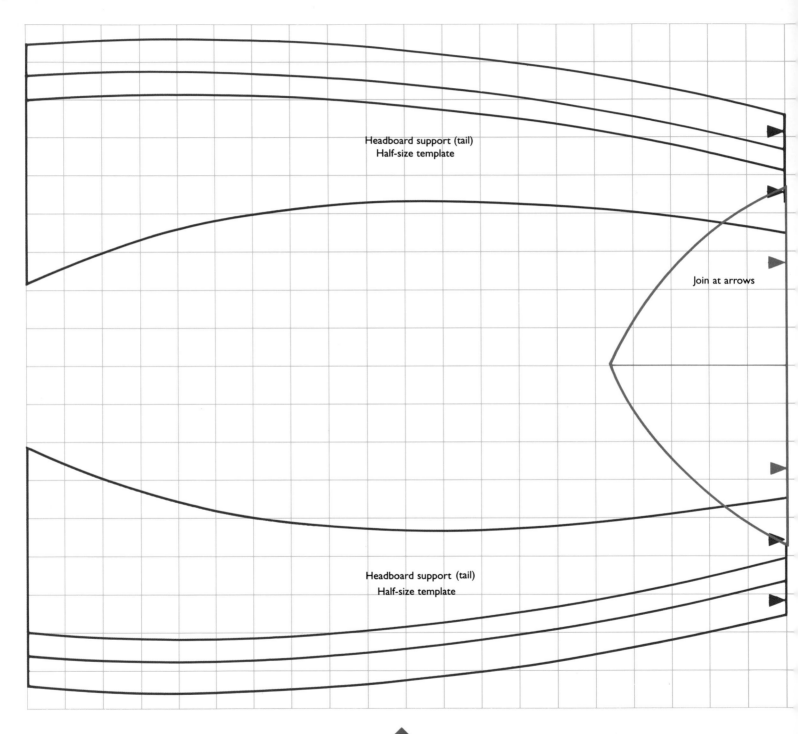

Headboard support (tail)
Half-size template

Join at arrows

Headboard support (tail)
Half-size template

Templates

Scale these templates up or use them straight from the page to make the heads and tails.

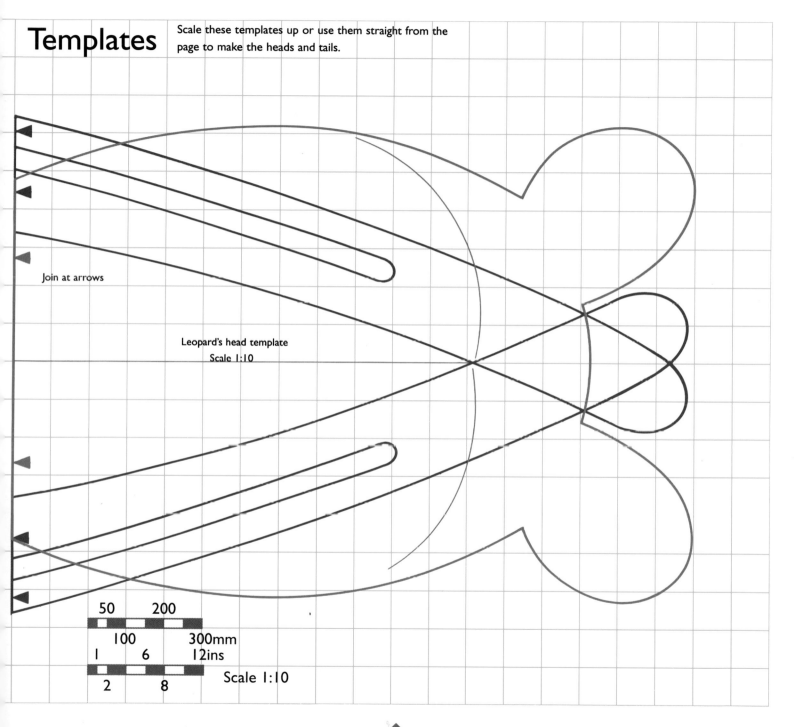

Join at arrows

Leopard's head template
Scale 1:10

50   200
100   300mm
1   6   12ins
2   8   Scale 1:10

Cutting the shapes

1 First gather the components for each of the two cats – a long piece for the main body, four legs, a head, a tail, and other blocks shown in the illustrations to thicken and build the shapes of the body and limbs. Cut the inside curve first to give the legs their correct stance.

3 Once you have a good fit, apply the glue and cramp the blocks in place.

2 Add the blocks that make the shoulders to the front of the legs, and start fitting the flanks behind the legs.

4 The outsides of the legs are curved, so you need to use the pieces of waste from the insides of the legs and glue and cramp them to the outsides of the legs.

5 Cut an angled recess in both sides of the main body piece at the rear and glue and cramp both legs in position.

6 Cut two more thickening pieces for the back legs and glue and cramp these in position as before. At this stage the animal is a plank for the back with four legs and some local thickening attached.

The head and tail

7 Next, mark out the head and tail. You can either use your own design drawn directly on the wood or trace round a template. Carefully cut out the shape.

8 Now cut the tail, which is curved, and rout a groove parallel to the curved front edge. Remember that this groove needs to be on the inside when the two animals are standing together, so that the headboard can be fitted in place. Note the

adaptation of a straight fence to enable you to rout parallel with a curved component. In this case two pieces of dowel are cut in half to make two half rounds and fitted to the fence to enable the machine to follow a curve.

9 Complete this groove and put the two tails to one side to be fixed later.

Shaping the body

10 The photographs show the use of a fairly recently developed power carving tool. It is similar to an angle grinder but has a special cutter that fits in place of the grinding wheel. If you decide to use this, remember that great care must be taken. Always ensure that both you and the work are securely placed and stable, and wear goggles to protect your eyes from splinters and dust. If you do not have such a tool you can use carving gouges throughout. Carve major waste from the blocks and continue carving to bring the shape as close as possible to the one you wish to achieve.

11 You will see that it is useful not to have the tail in position at this stage, since the body can be turned in all directions to allow you to work more easily.

12 Continue with this shaping and then use the same basic procedure with the head.

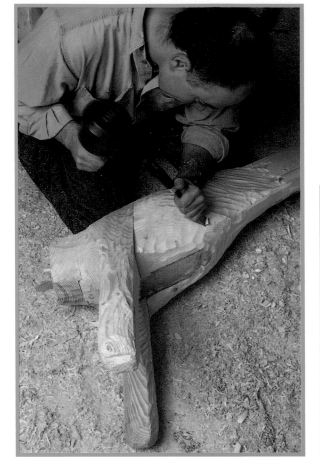

13 If you are using the power carving tool, stop when the baulk is near the final shape and carry out the final carving with a gouge. At this stage you have more control to achieve a really fine finish; let the gouge marks be a part of the surface texture and decoration. Work in the same way on the head as you have with the body.

14 To fix the head to the body, mark the position of the dowels between the body and head. Drill the holes and insert the dowels.

15 If necessary, clean up the edges at this point with a plane. Now glue the head in place.

Shaped face

16 When the glue has dried, carry out some final carving with the grinder and use gouges until the front is finished.

17 When all the carving is complete you can fix the tail in place. A way of ensuring the dowels are in the correct position is to put some pins on one joint face to locate the pins in position; gently press both faces together and those pins will give you an exact register on the opposing face.

18 Remove the pins and drill the holes to accept the dowels. Put the dowels in the holes and glue the tail in position. You now have two cats ready to decorate.

20 Decorate the headboard by etching a design of your choice on the surface and then painting over it.

19 Make the headboard from a sheet of plywood. Cut a series of lateral grooves on the reverse side to make it easier to bend the wood. Cut two tapered curved battens and glue and cramp these in position on the ply to hold the curve of the headboard.

Decorating

21 Paint the base coat, in this case yellow, on the body and face; continue until you have painted both animals completely. Now add the details.

22 An interesting effect can be achieved by using a small blowtorch to scorch the surface to create the animal's spots.

23 Alternatively, you can use paint to apply the markings and any facial features.

Assembly

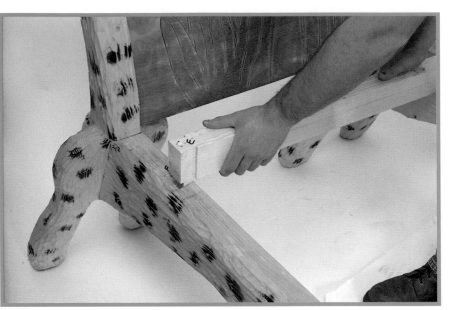

24 To link the cross rails of the bed, first make a lapped dovetail where each crossrail joins the sides and cut with a saw. Then remove the waste by drilling out and chiselling to the marked lines.

27 The completed assembly should be extremely solid and sturdy at this stage.

25 Drill and countersink screw holes in the crossrails, then slot the crossrails into the sides of the animal supports. Slot the headboard into the grooves between the tails.

28 Fit a perforated sheet of manufactured board on the crossrails, add some cosy bedding and you'll soon persuade even your most boisterous child that it's bedtime.

26 Now secure the assembly firmly using very long screws or bolts through the rails and the body supports.

Beautiful Beds

This project was based on a leopard but there are many other animals that your child could choose. Experiment with different body shapes and sizes. This is a full-size single bed but, if space is limited, you can always scale it down to a smaller size to suit a younger child.

Ancient Egypt Following the theme used in projects like the storage unit, this sphinx design works well and a lot can be done by painting pyramids on the headboard to reinforce the theme. Don't forget to adapt the feet of the bed to whatever design you choose, as shown in the three examples on this page.

Racing Car For something a little more sporty, why not try this racing car design? The four wheels could be made using the same principles as for the shelving unit with recesses for the bed support. Then you can decorate the headboard in your child's favourite team colours.

Alligator This variation on the animal theme means a subtle change of body shape to a more squat design for an alligator or crocodile. This approach gives you an opportunity not only to change the decoration for the body, but also to try out different shapes for the feet.

Flora and Fauna Don't forget that, whatever type of animal you choose, you need to decorate the headboard to reflect its surroundings, as with this tiger hiding in long grass.

More Big Cats This tiger design is simple and similar to the original. Paint stripes instead of spots, not forgetting the head. Another alternative is a cheetah, with blotches rather than spots or stripes. This way, unlike the alligator above, the basic carved body shape can remain the same.

Circus Wardrobe

The number "10" appears in a diamond at top.

10

This design is a fresh approach for a child wanting more than a traditional wardrobe. The piece comprises: a base cabinet and drawers; four uprights containing three panels and a fitted curtain door; a top frame holding a pyramid fabric canopy. The whole piece is connected by wooden balls. It is simplest to make this piece by working on each component in turn. Start with the base cabinet which comprises a top, a bottom, two sides with grooves and a back.

TOOLS

Hand	Power	Machine	Function
Panel saw	circular/jigsaw	radial arm saw/ dimension saw	cut panels
Plane	electric plane	surfacer/ thicknesser	plane materials
Plough or rebate plane	router		cut grooves
	Biscuit jointer		make carcase joints
	(or make routered grooves and use ply tongues)		
Mallet and hammer			fit joints
Sash cramps			cramp joints
Wheelbrace/brace	electric drill	pillar drill	drill holes
Twist drills, auger or spade bits, twist bits, forstner bits			drill holes
		Lathe	turn balls (or purchase already turned)
Screwdriver			insert screws
Brushes/mops		spray gun	apply finish

CUTTING LIST

Part	No	Length	Width	Thickness
From manufactured board				
Base cabinet top	1	545mm	520mm	15mm
		21½in	20½in	⅝in
Cabinet bottom	1	545mm	545mm	15mm
		21½in	21½in	⅝in
Cabinet sides	2	535mm	370mm	15mm
		21in	14½in	⅝in
Cabinet back	1	500mm	370mm	15mm
		19¾in	14½in	⅝in
Drawer bases	3	485mm	440mm	6mm
		19⅛in	17½in	¼in
Drawer sides	6	520mm	108mm	12mm
		20½in	4¼in	½in
Drawer backs	3	440mm	108mm	12mm
		17½in	4¼in	½in
Drawer fronts	3	470mm	108mm	12mm
		18½in	4¼in	½in
False drawer fronts	3	510mm	115mm	15mm
		20in	4½in	⅝in

Part	No	Length	Width	Thickness
From solid wood				
Base cabinet lippings	6	545mm	30mm	15mm
		21½in	1¼in	⅝in
Drawer runner inserts	6	535mm	28mm	9mm
		21in	1⅛in	⅜in
Drawer runners	6	520mm	15mm	9mm
		20½in	⅝in	⅜in
Side curved uprights	4	1415mm	42mm	35mm
		4ft 7⅝in	1⅝in	1⅜in
Top frame main members	4	800mm	55mm	42mm
		2ft 7½in	2⅛in	1⅝in
Top frame pyramid sides	4	480mm	15mm	12mm
		19in	⅝in	½in
Frame central boss	1	65mm		65mm diam.
		2½in		2½in diam.
Balls	9	65mm diam.		
		2½in diam.		
Hanging rail	1	700mm		22mm diam.
		27½in		⅞in diam.
Rail supports	2	100mm	65mm	20mm
		4in	2½in	¾in

Part	No	Length	Width	Thickness
From plywood				
Side panels	2	1422mm	518mm	6mm
		4ft 8in	20⅜in	¼in
Back panel	1	1422mm	708mm/518mm	6mm
			(top/bottom)	
		4ft 8in	27⅞in/20⅜in	¼in
			(top/bottom)	

Plus: Offcuts of 15mm (⅝in) MDF for handles, offcuts of 22mm (⅞in) dowel for handle supports, 6mm (¼in) chromed steel rod, curtain rings, fabric, glue, screws/male threaded inserts, female threaded inserts, clear lacquer, paints, abrasive paper, biscuits joints or ply tongues.

Plans and Elevations

100   400

200   600mm
2   12   24ins
4   16

Scale 1:20

Side elevation

Front elevation

Plan

Exploded views

The base cabinet

1 First mark out the components on the board material, using a T-square against a straight edge and marking with pencil and ruler.

2 The top and bottom are made from manufactured board – in this case MDF – and have solid wood lippings on some edges. The top has lippings on the front and back, while the bottom has lippings all round. Prepare these two components first by making a groove in the edge of the MDF where a lipping will be fitted.

3 Then machine the solid lipping to make a tongue that will fit into this groove.

4 Mark the solid wood to length, allowing for a mitre on each of the four corners. These can be cut either from the saw or, for greater accuracy, trim using a mitre shooting board with a plane.

5 Now glue the lippings onto the MDF and cramp in place.

6 When the glue is dry, plane the lipping flush with the MDF, noting that the overall dimension of the top is smaller than that of the bottom.

CROSS REFERENCE

Reading drawings	9
Routing	14
Planing	13

The sides and back

7 The back is plain but the sides need grooves in them into which the drawer runners will fit. It is generally not advisable to run drawer runners directly on manufactured board, so insert strips of solid timber into the board face where the grooves for the drawer runners will be cut. Start by making a series of routered cuts to accept these solid strips.

9 Now rout the grooves into these strips to take the drawer runners in the correct position.

8 Then apply glue to the groove and tap in the strips. When the glue is dry, plane these strips flush with the MDF face.

10 The cabinet is connected with biscuit joints, so make the necessary slots in the top and bottom edges of the sides and back.

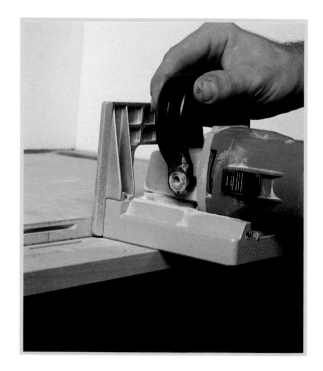

11 Make the corresponding slots in the inside faces of the top and bottom and, at the same time, make a groove in the bottom that will accept the side and back panels. When this is complete, check the whole assembly dry and, if all is well, prepare for final assembly.

13 Now assemble the bottom, top, two sides and back, making sure that the cabinet is square when the joints are cramped.

12 Place the biscuits in their slots and apply glue to the joint area. Note that a hole has been drilled at the corners which will secure the uprights.

The drawers

14 Now make the drawers to fit into the cabinet. These can be made in MDF in a similar way. Each drawer has one bottom, two sides, one back and one front, so cut these to size. Note that the sides, backs and fronts need grooves on the inside to accept the drawer bottom.

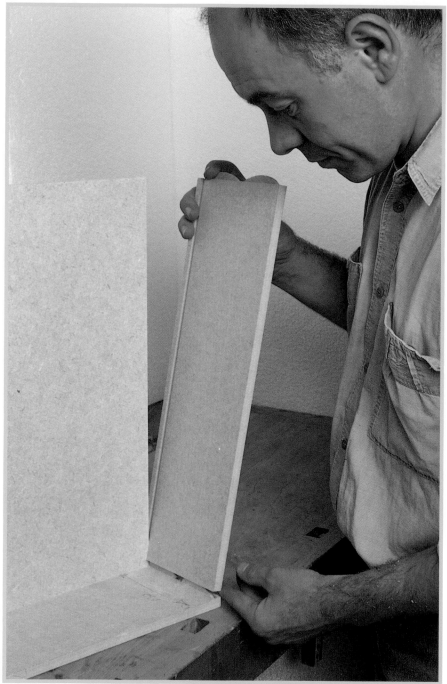

15 Make the joints between the bottom, sides and back and assemble.

16 Cut grooves in the sides that will accept the drawer runners. The drawer fronts are applied separately, so make them now and fit them later (see step 25). Make these runners on which the drawers will slide and fit them into the grooves. You can then run the drawers in the cabinet.

The uprights

17 First cut the uprights to size and then make a series of grooves for the side and back panels to sit in. Note that the two rear uprights will need a groove on the two inside faces, while the front two uprights only need one groove each on an inside face. Then drill the ends so that the threaded inserts that will hold the balls can be fitted. Many hardware stores should sell connectors that have a machine screw thread on one end and a wood screw thread on the other.

18 Now make the wooden balls for the feet and tops of the frame. The sequence shows these being made in the lathe. First turn the wood into a cylinder and then start to work that into a sphere.

19 When you have achieved this, drill the end of the ball in the lathe to accept the special threaded insert. Make sure that the thread on this insert is identical on the inserts that went into the ends of the uprights.

20 You should find that these inserts can be screwed into place using an Allen key, and you can now assemble the uprights to the base unit using four balls that will become the wardrobe's feet.

CROSS REFERENCE

Joints	14
Wood turning	12
Fixings	15

21 To make the top frame, cut the timber to size and make the mitred halving. Assemble this frame and, when the glue is dry, trim all round with a plane. Then mark and drill the holes on the corner.

22 Turn this unit over and rout a groove in three sides to accept the side/back panels.

23 Cut the four strips for the pyramid edges and make the central boss, in this case a turned cylinder with a sloping top into which the pyramid edges are joined. Make and fit this joint and fit this component to the frame.

24 This is a good time to make the fabric canopy. Mark out four triangles and scalloped edges in paper and tape these in position over the frame. Transfer the shapes to the fabric and cut out the pieces, remembering to leave allowances for seams. Sew the pieces together to make the canopy, leaving a hole at the corners to allow the wooden balls to be screwed in. Check the hood for fit and remove.

26 Again from offcuts, shape two rectangles to make holders for the hanging rail and drill a hole partway through each large enough for the dowel or broomstick. Drill and countersink two screw holes in each holder.

25 Cut three shapes of your choice from offcuts of 15mm (⅝in) solid wood for the drawer handles, and three cylindrical pieces to connect them to the drawers. Smooth all pieces to finish and glue each handle and cylinder assembly to a drawer front. These pieces could be painted before assembly. Then fit the drawer fronts and handles to the drawers themselves.

CROSS REFERENCE	
Routing	14
Joints	14

Assembly

27 Mark out and cut the ply for the back and sides and fit the back and then the sides, clamping in place, locating in the grooves cut in the uprights.

28 You can now assemble the piece. Secure the pyramid to the frame and fit the top frame to the assembly using another four balls.

29 To decorate the sides, mark out your decoration and paint the background yellow. Apply the red for the nose and trousers, then add the blue stripes to the trousers. Add the shirt, braces and bow tie, and then the clown's features and hair. Complete the picture with a silly hat and big boots.

30 If you wish, add outlines and details and allow the work to dry. Using a brush or spray, you can now add a clear coat of varnish to seal the work and complete the side. Paint the back in a colour of your choice.

31 Now make the curtain closure from the same material used for the canopy. Cut two rectangles of white material and turn the edges under. Then cut two narrow dark strips, turn the edges under all round, and sew these on top of the white material. Sew strips of ribbon along the top on the reverse side.

32 Glue and reassemble all the non-glued parts. Screw the two rail holders inside each side, with the dowel or broomstick in place between them. Relocate the side panels in place.

33 Thread the curtain rings onto the wire rod and fix this inside the front uprights in the holes that you have drilled. Then glue or fasten the canopy in place over the frame, place the frame on top of the uprights and screw the five wooden balls in place. To finish, tie the ribbons onto the curtain rings to hang the curtains.

Magical Wardrobes

The main theme here was the circus and the easiest way to change the look is by painting different images on the sides. Another approach is altering the drawer arrangements and changing them to match the alternative suggestions for the desk and stool set.

Colours and Cutouts
These also work well, especially when a heart theme is used. The unit also looks good in strong, bold colours in stripes as used on the desk and stool set in project 2.

Base Variations
Another effective approach is to change the under-storage from drawers to open shelves, a cupboard with hinged doors or a cupboard with a hinged fall.

The Royal This wardrobe looks excellent with a crown and golden orbs, heraldic devices on the side, lion's feet on the bottom and more heraldic symbols on the drawer handles.

Index

a, b, c, d, e after a number refer to columns in the introductory section.

Credits

Quarto and the author would like to thank all the furniture makers for their contributions and also the parents and guardians of the following children: Timothy Dixon, Jemma and Sophie Heseltine, Samson Jayes, Chloë Keeves and Madeleine Phillips. Props supplied by Pat Byrne, Jo Carlill, Anna French Ltd, London and Susannah Jayes. Thanks also to Kate Robinson, Raye Simpson and Lulu Sturdy.